Married To The Vent

An Autobiography

By

Carl Philip Holmes ·

authorHOUSE™

1663 LIBERTY DRIVE, SUITE 200
BLOOMINGTON, INDIANA 47403
(800) 839-8640
WWW.AUTHORHOUSE.COM

First published by AuthorHouse 06/30/05

ISBN: 1-4208-2999-8 (sc)

Printed in the United States of America
Bloomington, Indiana

This book is printed on acid-free paper.

<u>FOREWORD</u>

The reason for calling my book, "Married to the Vent," is because the marriage vows go something like this; "For richer or poorer, in sickness and in health, till death us do part!" Also, being married can be a pain in the neck, just like my vent!

So don't have an accident or a stroke, otherwise you'll end up like me, the poor bloody bloke!

This book is about my life now, and before my stroke. I will take you on a journey through my life, until today……

CARL HOLMES
MARRIED TO THE VENT
AN AUTOBIOGRAPHY

I was born on the 3rd October 1973 in Colchester, Essex and was very unwell. My parents and the doctors thought I wouldn't survive. I was underweight and they discovered that I had an extra (3rd) kidney. This extra kidney lay dormant and eventually 'disappeared' of its own accord. I struggled and survived. Mum and Dad divorced sometime during 1974/5, when I was only three months old. I was

1

brought up on the Greenstead Estate in Colchester and lived with my Mum, who in 1974 met and set up home with Mark. My Dad and Grandmother who lived in Halstead brought up my older brother Stephen who visited us in Colchester every fortnight. I would also visit my dad's house and my Nan's house in Halstead.

In 1977 I started at the local primary school, Hazelmere School, where quite often my reports commented, "Must try harder!" I progressed through the junior school and on to Sir Charles Lucas Comprehensive where I flunked out, as all I wanted to do was work. It never occurred to me that school had anything to do with my future in the workplace.

My brother Darren was born in 1975 and Toby followed in 1977. They both followed in my footsteps through the local schools but completed their education with Darren getting a Maths Degree at Essex University. Today Darren is a maths teacher at Charles Lucas Comprehensive School, and Toby passed an apprenticeship in motor mechanics and now works for Nissan.

My older brother Stephen left school at 16 without any qualifications and has had a wide variety of jobs and is still living in Halstead.

Darren, Toby and I were brought up together and shared a loving brotherly relationship, but of course we used to fight and argue as brothers do! Throughout my childhood I've got up to many little pranks and as my circle of friends grew the pranks became more frequent. One of the friends I made at primary school is Dean Binks and he is still my friend.

As I grew up I spent most of my free time with Darren, Toby and our friends. Dean and I were very close and we got up to many foolish escapades. We often went to St. Osyth, a beach near Clacton-on-Sea with our parents and used to enjoy ourselves in the amusement arcades. Darren, Dean and I joined the Scouts and went camping, where we got up to mischief as you do when you are kids. The family went on our first holiday abroad in 1987 and we went to Corfu, which was a bit of a disaster as we all got food poisoning and badly sun burnt. Later in 1988, my sister Kelly was born and another sister called Lucy in 1991.

When I reached the age of 17 I took my first driving lesson and I passed my test, first time, after only fifteen lessons. Prior to passing my test I had bought my first car, a little MG Metro. I was so overjoyed when I passed my test that I ran down the path of my house with my thumbs in the air, all my family were very pleased for me. My brother Darren then persuaded me to take him for a little test drive. I was not too keen at first but eventually gave in. I took him for a little drive in Wivenhoe and he persuaded me to let him have a drive. We got about 100 yards down the road when he misjudged the distance between us and a parked car and damaged the bumper, which we ended up having to pay for! Darren too, eventually passed his driving test, after he had taken proper driving lessons with a qualified driving instructor!

I made many friends when I started going to town in my car and had many girlfriends. I was working for my stepdad Mark who had his own business in contract cleaning. I eventually changed my job to work for the Ministry of Defence as a labourer. I got this job through a contact that I made during the time I was working for Mark.

During 1992 I started suffering with mild depression and unfortunately in 1994 I was made medically retired from the M.O.D. Although I was expecting it, I was still disappointed to become unemployed.

During 1993 I used to go out in my car every evening with friends I made in Colchester, especially Dean, we used to stay out until all hours. Dean, bought his first house in Highwoods, and I bought a flat nearby, but after a few months I found I couldn't afford to keep it, even though I used to have a second job at weekends at a local hotel where I was made redundant after 6 months.

I eventually traded in my MG Metro for an XR2 and I often used to see my Metro still going about. One day the new owner of my old MG Metro flagged me down and I got talking to him and he said, "I know who you are, you used to own the car before me, didn't you?" I said to him that I got rid of it because it kept playing me up and I had already had to buy another engine for it. And he then said to me "Yes, I have had nothing but trouble with it as well." I could not help but laugh, especially when he told me that since he's had it he has had 3 engines for it! I often used to wave to him when I saw him, as I would recognise my old car anywhere.

I eventually smashed the XR2 one frosty morning and I decided to get rid of it. I traded in my XR2 for a Nova SR that was newer. I could no longer keep my flat or my car when I lost my weekend job and eventually lost the mortgage and my flat was repossessed. I went to live with my friend Dean for a couple of months. Then I moved back to live in my mother's house in Colchester, which I shared with Darren and Toby, as Mum, Mark and my two sisters had moved to Chelmsford because of Mark's work. For a short time my brother Steve moved in with us and then moved on as he always does, he went to live in London and worked in a pub.

In 1995, while still suffering with depression, I started evening classes at Greyfriars Adult Education doing computers and lived on benefits. I was feeling a bit low, and decided to take a break and go on holiday for two weeks in May. I visited Rome, Barcelona, Corsica, Elba and Monte Carlo where I visited the Formula One-track circuit. I stayed for a week in Magaluf, Spain where I made a few friends, going out drinking and clubbing. I got badly burnt which is not unusual with my fair skin. After the holiday I returned to my studies and continued to go out with my friends, Dean and Steve. We visited clubs, the casino in Southend, went to London, shopping and clubbing, and often liked a bet on the horses and playing snooker.

I eventually took up weight training at Uncle Norman's gym and followed a strict diet to build up the muscles. I trained everyday for two hours with a strict diet taking protein amino acid tablets for about 6 months. However, on the night of December 12th 1996 I was rushed to hospital after collapsing during a training session. I had complained of pains in the back of my neck. My uncle rubbed some cream in and I carried on training, then I had a twinge in the back of my neck and started running around screaming saying, "I can't breathe!" My uncle phoned for an ambulance. Before the ambulance arrived, Toby and Juliet, who was a lodger at that time, arrived on the scene, summoned by Uncle Norman within minutes to comfort me. As soon as the paramedics arrived I collapsed at their feet unconscious. From then I can't remember what happened until I regained consciousness in ITU at Adenbrookes Hospital a few days later.

I was told that when I was transferred from Colchester Hospital to Adenbrookes ITU, the paramedics in the ambulance had to revive me using "electric shock".

I awoke in ITU with a tube down my throat to help me breathe, but I was told that I was continually biting it (I do remember that) so I had a tracheotomy performed to let me breathe with the help of a ventilator.

When I woke up again, I couldn't see or move any bit of my body apart from blinking my eyelids. I remember hearing a nurses voice saying "Hello, darling", and stoking my head but I couldn't see or speak to her. I think it was a couple of days before I started to regain consciousness, hearing this "lovely voice" of a nurse called Jane who kept comforting me. When my family came in to see me, they said "Carl – can you blink your eyes if you can hear me". Then they knew that I could hear and understand them and they told me that they would go through the alphabet and that I could blink at the letters I needed to spell words to make a sentence. This was a long process to communicate but we had to do that from then on.

Several days later I was able to open my mouth, my tongue and mouth were totally covered with a thick, dry and crusty film of secretion, which I kept trying to scrape off with my teeth. When I was eventually able to move my mouth muscle, I decided to grimace at the letters instead of blinking. My mother and brother Stephen went to Burger King and bought chicken nuggets and fed me to see if I could eat and swallow, as they were told I would never be able to swallow. I proved them wrong! I managed to eat one chicken nugget. I was actually being fed through a nasogastric tube for about a month before I started taking fluid by a syringe, and also topped up regularly through the nasogastric tube.

I must explain that a tracheostomy is the surgical procedure when doctors make the temporary or permanent opening in the trachea (the pipe that takes the air to the lungs) and a tracheostomy is the incision (hole) that doctors make to receive the ventilator pipe into the trachea.

Eventually I started to make noises through a cuffed tracheostomy tube. The air in the tracheostomy balloon is let down to enable me to learn to talk again, about three times a day for a minute at a time. I could only make screaming noises as I lost the ability to speak, then they would inflate the balloon again. I couldn't make any sound at all with the cuff inflated. However, one day a nurse came in and said to me that if it was a nice day tomorrow, she would take me down to see the ducks. But they didn't know that now and again my cuff would slightly deflate a bit so I could talk. When the nurse came back she was very surprised to hear me speaking. I then replied to her question by saying, "Fuck the ducks! I don't even like them".

Eventually I was transferred to Colchester ITU where I laid on an airbed, which used to rock from side to side and give percussion; it was designed for chest physio. Not long after, I had the cuffed tracheostomy taken out and replaced with an uncuffed one.

I was learning to talk again, but it was very difficult especially having to talk with the ventilator as the breath goes in and over the vocal cords. I will now take you through a little section of ventilation and I will also do the same with every subject that I mention, which may be unknown to others.

VENTILATION

The ventilator is a machine designed to either help you breathe or to assist with your own breathing. I have been on a few different types of ventilators. Firstly starting with a ventilator called a Caesar. This ventilator is particularly used in ITU and is a big machine where the tidal volume is adjusted to suit your needs and lung capacity, which is also decided by an anaesthetist. The Caesar ventilator has three alarms. 1. Low Pressure, which is when you have been disconnected, or there is a leak. 2. High Pressure, which is when you have a blockage, or you need suction or if the tube is kinked. The third alarm will sound if you are not helping the ventilator initiate breaths. When the alarm sounds it is letting you know that you are not helping but it will still give the breath. When this used to alarm the nurses would shout out "Come on Carl breathe", and I would have to try and concentrate to breathe.

When I was in Papworth I was given a ventilator called a Puritan Bennett. My tidal volume in the beginning was only 675 litres of air, which was quite low, but at the time it seemed to suit me and I didn't have to do any breathing for myself. Somewhere along the line my breathing capability had deteriorated and the mode I was on was called "Control". This means that the ventilator is doing the breathing by itself, without my help. I took the same ventilator to Stoke Mandeville but gradually increased the tidal volume to suit my lung capacity. This ventilator also has a breath rate (which is how many breaths I am getting a minute). In Papworth I was on 8 breaths per minute and there was also another setting called High Alarm and Low Alarm. The high alarm setting was set on 50 and this would alarm if the pressure reached this high. The high-pressure alarm is caused by heavy secretions, blocked trachea or kinked circuit. The low-pressure alarm was set on 14 and this would alarm if I became disconnected at either the trachea end or the ventilator end or if there is a split in the tubing.

My tidal volume is now on 1.4 litres and my breath rate 14 breaths per minute, and the lower alarm is now set on 12. This is because for the past year or so I have been sleeping with my mouth open, so the air escapes and when I reached 14 it used to alarm and

7

drive me round the bend. Now when I sleep with my mouth open it doesn't actually reach as low as 12 so it doesn't alarm. I'm still on the same ventilator and the same settings today. Additionally there is a filter on the back of the ventilator, which is changed monthly, and the circuit tubing is changed weekly. At the tracheostomy end is a catheter mount and an HME filter. The catheter mount is changed alternate days but was changed daily during my stay at Stoke Mandeville. The HME filter is changed daily and HME stands for Heat and Moisture Exchange.

The ventilator circuit and tubing is connected to the tracheostomy, which is placed in my trachea. The breath goes through the tracheostomy tube and into my lungs. The tracheostomy which I use is a size 8 cuffless which has an inner tube which needs cleaning on a regular basis, otherwise this may block with sputum and stop the ventilation going down to my lungs. The tracheostomy, when I was in hospital was changed monthly, but now I live in the community this can go longer due to fewer bugs. You have to have a size 6 available just in case they are unable to get the size 8 in. Some people when their tracheostomy hole is new can easily begin to close up so you need a smaller size in case this happens. If by then the size 6 still won't go in you have to use a pair of tracheal dilators which hold the hole open to get the tracheotomy in, they look very similar to a pair of forceps. I'm still on 1.4 litres even today and also have all the same settings. After Colchester ITU I transferred to Papworth, which is a sleep centre and what they do is monitor everyone's breathing. I was transferred there to see if I could get off the ventilator.

While I was in Papworth they did a test on my breathing called a "Phrenic nerve test." This test is done with little probes that are placed near the phrenic nerve (just below the collar bone), these give out a little voltage, like an electric shock, which stimulates the nerve to help you breathe. These are hand-made in Finland and are very expensive. I was told that the pacemaker would work on me so I went to theatre, had the operation and then found out it wouldn't work, so they took it out and stitched me back up. The operation had failed. When I awoke I saw my family and I said to them "Did it work, am I breathing?" They started crying and they said, "Sorry

Carl, but it didn't work". I got upset, but I still tried to keep on top of it.

Where my scar was, I was given a little catheter bag, which is called a chest drain, which collects excess fluid and blood. This was eventually taken out and I was sewn back up. I still have the scar there today. When I was at Papworth I had an airbed, which had an air pillow and an air footrest that could easily be deflated if the deflate button was accidentally pulled, which happened to me on several occasions whilst in bed. I was in a unit with other patients with no staff in the ward at all apart from the nurses at the nurse station and, if my ventilator became disconnected, they would only arrive if the alarms went on my ventilator.

I also had a sats monitor, connected to my ear, this would alarm if my oxygen stats ratio dropped below 90% or if my pulse dropped below 54. Good oxygen saturation is between 95% - 100%. The way I was told to call a nurse was to drop my head to one side so the ear probe would fall off and make my stats machine alarm sound, which meant that it was disconnected. But to this day I cannot believe that I allowed myself to be on my own and to rely on alarms to get attention.

After about three months I was transferred to Stoke Mandeville, which was about June or July 1997. I was placed in a little side room in case I had caught the hospital bug MRSA. I was eventually moved into a four bedded bay called 'The Ventilator Bay' which always had 1-2 nurses there at all times. This bay had 4 ventilated patients, so if we were in trouble breathing or disconnected, there was always someone there. I stayed at Stoke Mandeville until 29th February 2000. During the time I was there I received intensive physiotherapy, which consisted of daily stretches on the arms and legs to maintain movement, so that the joints didn't seize up. I also used to stand on a tilt table, which is very good for spasms. This was a long bed with a footplate at the bottom. You have to lie on the bed and have several straps tie you down so that you don't fall off. They would then gradually raise the tilt table according to how high you could tolerate it, because some people, if they go up too high or up too quickly, would pass out or faint due to the drop in blood pressure. I would stand for approximately one hour and then be put back down again afterwards. This exercise is very good for spasm, as all your body weight would be on your legs just as if you were standing up normally, and this is very good for the circulation.

Also, while I was there they teach you many things about yourself, these consist of learning about your bladder and bowels, spasms and what causes them and how to break them, and medication for them, also about being verbally independent. This is to instruct people about your care and they also teach you about sexuality. While I was in Stoke Mandeville I learnt to use conveen sheath drainage. A lot of tetraplegics cannot pass urine by themselves. I was always told I was a unique case, as I can pass urine by myself. Most spinal injury patients have a catheter inserted into their penis, or a supapubic catheter, because they cannot pass urine by themselves or open their bowels – a lot of people have bowel care early in the morning, as this takes up quite a bit of the nurse's time in getting all the patients done. Most of these patients need suppositories and would lie on their left side and have a manual evacuation, which means that the nurse puts on a glove and eases out the stools with her finger until the lower bowel is empty. Because I have some control I use the bedpan with the help of suppositories, but occasionally I do need a manual evacuation.

A lot of spinal injury patients get spasms and the higher the level of injury you have the stronger the spasm, especially in the legs. The spine has many levels, starting from C1-8 then T1-12, L1-5 and then S1-5. Each person, with a spinal injury is different, but the majority of them experience similar effects. Most of them cannot feel or pass urine or empty their bowels by themselves, or feel pain, whereas I can feel all over. A lot of patients have to have pressure relief because they can't feel anything. This consists of rolling from side to side in bed or leaning forward in the chair. This stops red areas and sores arising. But while they are in hospital many of them build up a skin tolerance and they get to know when they should turn. Also a lot of these patients suffer from dysreflexia. This is a way of your body telling you there's pain somewhere. Normally if you have a problem with a full bladder or bowels or pressure sores or even an ingrown toenail, this would tell your body there's something wrong by producing either a thumping headache or high blood pressure. If you don't rectify the problem you could have a stroke.

ON THE SUBJECT OF SPASMS

Spasms are involuntary movements which are caused by a full bladder, full bowel, injury to toenails, or sitting on something like a zip. Many nurses advise you not to have buttons or zips on your clothes as they can mark your skin or cause a spasm. Spasms vary from patient to patient some are strong and some mild. I have seen some strong spasms which have caused someone's legs to fly in the air causing discomfort and pain. Some spasms could throw you out of a chair or bed. Spasms can be controlled by medication either Dantrolene, Baclofen tablets or a Baclofen pump, which is placed in the base of the stomach and has a wire which goes to the spinal cord discharging Baclofen into the spinal cord. This is a very effective way of controlling spasm but some people choose it while others don't. Spasms can be broken in the legs by bending the toes down. This is a very effective way of breaking a spasm in the legs. Some people get spasms in their arms, shoulders and neck, which causes ones head to rear over, also spasms can occur in the stomach and chest.

TRACHEOSTOMIES

Tracheostomies are little plastic tubes, which are situated at the base of the throat into your trachea, connected to this is ventilator tubing, connected to the ventilator. The ventilator gives a volume of air which pushes down the trachea into the lungs, which expand the lungs – artificial breathing. You will breathe as anyone else but at regulated breaths per minute. You can only talk when the air passes over the vocal cords. There is a device called a speaking valve, which you can use for a telephone conversation. This traps the air into a filter in the speaking valve so that you can talk for longer. You have a continual flow of air. This is not recommended for use all the time as it can bloat you out.

A lot of patients with a trache get heavy chest secretions, which need constant attention by a physiotherapist or trained nurse. They will shake your chest, percussion (banging) or chest physio, to loosen the secretions and then they would give you suction. Suction is a way of getting these secretions and the mucous from the chest. This is done by a suction catheter, which comes in many sizes to suite your trache. I have size 14. A suction catheter is totally sterile and pulled out of a sterile packet and only handled by a sterile glove and must not be contaminated. The patient's tracheostomy catheter mount is disconnected and the suction catheter is fed down the trache until it meets resistance. It is then pulled back about one inch and suction is applied until the majority of the secretions have been suctioned. Then there is a slow removal of catheter from trache.

You may have to repeat this several times until all secretions have been removed.

Constant cleaning of the inner tube, which is inside the trache, needs attention other wise the trache can become blocked off. If the inner tube is blocked off then a new trache has to be inserted under sterile conditions. The inner tube with a red base is a temporary one and this can only stay in for a short time whilst cleaning the other one. Tapes with Velcro hold in the tracheostomy and the trache dressing is positioned around the trache to collect loose secretions and this dressing needs changing every day. The other tapes need changing as necessary.

NEBULISERS

Nebulisers are used to loosen secretions on my chest when it is tight and difficult to breathe. This is a medication that goes into a nebuliser giving a set amount of medication, delivered down the tubing into the trachea using oxygen to nebulise. This enables more effective suctioning and chest physio. Nebulisers can also be "bagged in" or operated with a facial mask attached to a machine.

Bagging is also very essential if someone cannot breathe or if the ventilator has disconnected somewhere. It is a manual form of ventilation. It is a black or green balloon, which is squeezed in time with the normal breathing rate, not too fast otherwise the patient will hyperventilate. If a patient goes out for the day they must always take a spare trache kit, an ambu bag and a little portable suction machine with them. The tracheostomy kit must consist of a trache of your own size plus one a size smaller, and dilators, which will open the hole wider in case the trache won't go in. There is also KY jelly, tracheostomy tapes and dressing. In this emergency kit should be sterile gloves, sterile suction catheters and a spare inner tube.

THE PHYSIOTHERAPIST

The physiotherapist maintains stretches, legs, arms, head and chest physio. These stretches stop the joints from getting stiff and seizing up. There are certain ways that your limbs and joints need stretching and only the physiotherapist or trained parties know and are allowed to do these movements. The physiotherapist can also help your spasms by the use of a 'tilt table' or 'hydro therapy'. This comforts and relaxes the muscles and is very therapeutic. (More about physio further on.)

THE OCCUPATIONAL THERAPIST

The role of the Occupational Therapist is to get you fitted up for the right wheelchair, vehicle, hand splints and also additional things like computers and environmental controls. The hand splints are made using a hard nylon type plastic that is then heated in a pan, which moulds it into the shape of your hand. This is done over and over again until it is suitable to wear and leaves no marks on your skin. The hand splints are fastened onto the hand with Velcro straps, you would then build up a skin tolerance by wearing them gradually i.e. begin with half an hour and build up to longer times.

You would then also try out lots of wheelchairs to find out which one suits you better, this also applies to the cushion. This may take several weeks to find the right equipment. Most of this is at the Occupational Therapy Department or the Seating Clinic. You may also go to the Occupational Therapy Department to learn how to transfer in and out of a chair and a car. You may also learn about using the right computer for your needs.

It is likely that you will be offered the opportunity to try different vehicles that may be used by people who cannot transfer to and from a car. To get into a vehicle your wheelchair is placed on the chair lift which lifts you in your chair to the level of the back of the vehicle so that you can then be pushed into the vehicle, where your chair is locked into place.

Some people may receive an environmental control system in their home. This is a way of operating electrical appliances, such as lights, curtains and intercom, all controlled by voice or a switch.

Computers could also become a main part of your life. In the Occupational Therapy Department they will teach you how to use one using a switch or your own voice and, some people can also learn how to use one to write letters, answer the telephone or run a business. The Occupational Therapy Department will be involved in my being able to go out and about as they will train my family and friends to suction. This is an extremely good idea as I can then participate in family events and trips out. The same staff will initially show you how to "frog breathe." This is a very different way of learning how to breathe by lifting your neck muscles and at the same time gulping in air from the atmosphere. Some people can do this very effectively for hours while others are not so good at it and can only last a few minutes. This is very handy if you are in an emergency situation.

Many patients have a set daily routine, which may consist of having breakfast, washing, doing their ablutions and opening their bowels. They may also decide to have a shower, which can be a lengthy ordeal, as you have to be transferred to a shower trolley, or you may be able to use a shower chair. Once dried you may decide to go to bed as showering can make you hypothermic. Once you have warmed up you can transfer to your chair and start your daily routines and activities.

When I am transferred into my wheelchair it takes quite a while for me to get comfortable as I can feel every crease but, once comfortable I stay put for anything up to eight to ten hours a day. Some patients are pushed in their wheelchair by their carers and others can do it for themselves. They may use a power chair operated either by hand or chin controls and the speed is adjusted to individual needs and what you personally feel happy with.

I have used a power chair and get on quite well even though I am registered blind, but my eyesight has gradually improved whereas just after my accident I could not see a thing. I also have movement in my right thumb and index finger and can clench my fist, but I have no movement in my left hand at all. I have used my right hand to operate some machines and switches but it is very difficult and very tiring.

The same procedure applies for me getting comfortable in my bed as well as in my chair. I can feel everything all over so positioning takes a long time. Once I am comfortable I stay in the same position all night. I have come across many different types of nurses and that means that I have met some with very little patience with their patient! This can cause the patient a great deal of distress and frustration. But I must say there are very many that are extremely patient and listen to your instructions. This is very satisfying and makes me feel safe.

My brother Stephen is very bitter about my situation and will not accept what cannot be changed! Due to his distress he has upset many staff and other patients, but I understand that he can't help himself. There have been many occasions when Stephen has been near to causing a fight in a restaurant with staff! When he visited the atmosphere in the hospital changed. Although he has a temper I can see that he has a sensitive side with a great sense of humour. I don't see Stephen often as he moves from place to place and job to job and I rarely know where he is.

Since the accident I have seen several psychologists in Stoke Mandeville who have tried to comfort me and get me through the difficulties of coping with the way I am. Some were very helpful and some not, but they were also there to give advice and support to family and friends.

During my time in Stoke Mandeville I met several foreign nurses, some Spanish, Italian, Portuguese, German and Japanese and gradually I began to pick up a little of their languages. Some phrases were polite and useful but others were swear words, which I thought was quite comical. I did tend to use these words especially with the ones who had taught me them! We did have a good laugh. I still remember most of the words now.

Whilst I was in Stoke Mandeville I got to know lots of the staff and patients from other wards and I did make a lot of friends that were patients. Unfortunately, many of them have actually died now from chest infections or similar things. I must admit this has upset me a lot and I have had some bad episodes of depression because of these events. This is because they were my friends and I think that maybe this could happen to me, but I have still kept on top of it and I will never forget them.

Whilst at Stoke Mandeville I have had several episodes of memory loss and slight fits and it is very frustrating because my short-term memory gets very confused. After I have chatted with someone I can forget the conversation took place and repeat the questions again. This can be quite upsetting for my family. There was one occasion when my long-term memory went as well and I had to be transferred to St. Francis ward, for 'high dependency' patients. I can remember waking up there one night and being unable to remember who I was, where I was and why I couldn't move! I remember calling out and asking, "Where am I?" and a voice calling back telling me to go back to sleep, "You have had an accident, go back to sleep!" It was very distressing. I still occasionally have problems with my short-term memory but certainly not as bad as at the beginning.

I do have to be careful about unhealthy visitors as I can catch infections quite quickly and for me the consequences are dangerous, and even fatal. Since my accident I have had several chest infections, bouts of pneumonia, MRSA and sometimes the chest infection and the memory loss seem to be connected. MRSA is quite a problem as I then have to be in isolation, washed in a special disinfectant and the trachea site has to be cleaned very carefully. Whoever comes near me must be wearing rubber gloves and aprons that must be removed before going to the next patient.

During my time at Stoke Mandeville I was able to go on many outings using the "Paravan," a disabled van with a tail lift at the back. I went to the cinema, restaurants, especially Chinese, local pubs and concerts. We even went to the Natural History Museum in London where we spent the day looking round and I particularly enjoyed the dinosaurs. During the visit I saw a nice looking little café, which was not crowded where I thought we could have a bite to eat and drink. When I got to the till I realised why there were so few people there, the cost of three sandwiches and three coffees was extortionate! Still, that's the price of visiting London. But, we did have a good time. What I did find humorous was the Earthquake Simulator, which was a big room and once inside the door closed and the whole room shook from side to side and up and down. My wheelchair was going 10 to the dozen and so was my head! My portable suction machine fell on the floor, my ventilator tube popped off and fell on the floor and so did my head rest. Fred, one of my nurses, was running around trying to pick them all up whilst being thrown around himself. When we came out Fred and Gordon, the other nurse, were panting and out of breath and their hair was all over the place, where they had been thrown about. I was in hysterics and they both said, " You can bloody laugh – never again mate!" I also had a Japanese exchange student nurse called Eri who enjoyed the episode, and since she has left Stoke Mandeville she still writes to me.

I have mentioned before how persuasive Darren is and his talents were called into play again during my stay at Stoke Mandeville. There was a rather nice nurse called Joy, who Darren took a fancy to – but she refused to go out with him. You've got it, he persisted. Darren proposed one day in the ventilator bay, he got down on bended knee, in front of patients and visitors, pulled out a ring and asked Joy to marry him. Today she is his wife and my sister-in-law! They were married at St Andrews Church, Colchester, it was a wonderful day, the reception was at the Mill Hotel and I thoroughly enjoyed it.

Toby has also had romantic interludes with various nurses during my stays in hospital, one from Papworth who he doesn't see anymore, and another from Stoke Mandeville with whom he has a very good friendship. She came with him to Darren's wedding. Darren and Joy now have a beautiful baby daughter called Juliette, who I love to bits. Every time she sees me she sits on my lap and smiles at me.

After being together for nearly 25 years mum and Mark separated. It was such a shock for me as he has been like a father to me. I was extremely depressed. Throughout my stay in hospital I have had many episodes of depression and have thought about suicide on many occasions. In fact I tried on several occasions when I tried to knock my vent tube off with my chin. I have had a lot of counselling from psychologists, which I have found very helpful.

I can remember that even before my accident I suffered from depression on numerous occasions.

After a while mum and Mark got back together again and decided they would cement their relationship by marrying. I went to the wedding and just like at Darren's, I made a speech. I even mentioned their extremely long engagement – 25 years long! They were married in Great Baddow and the reception was held at the school where Mark is now a caretaker. It was a lovely day.

Toby had had a few drinks and got very emotional when it was time for me to return to the hospital, but by the time I got back he was on the phone saying he was feeling better and that he was looking forward to when I came home.

I have met some very interesting people during my hospitalisation and one of the auxiliary nurses from Papworth is now an air hostess who travels all over Europe, and when she has time she still visits me. She has told me that she would like to go back into nursing and to qualify.

Although I can't remember my accident I can still visualise events before the accident. Things like my bedroom and what was in it, my car, my friends, the places we visited, even the streets, and road signs. I can see them all in my head. Often when I am in bed I imagine myself at home, walking down the roads, going to the shopping centre, in my house, it seems so real to me. It feels like yesterday! It is funny how my long-term memory is not affected, but my short-term memory comes and goes.

Being on a ventilator and disabled the way I am is worrying and scary. I must admit even though I am generally very cheerful and happy I still do worry and fear for the worst. I often sit here and think about how long I am going to live and how I am going to die. On numerous occasions I have had episodes where I have come off the vent and help has not come quickly. Several times when my trachea has blocked off and when I can't breath I wonder, "Carl, how do you think you are going to die?" I hate thinking about it and hate giving myself an answer. I would hate to die from lack of ventilation, as not being able to breathe is horrifying and you can't explain how this feels and what you go through at the time. I also fear and worry when my family leaves me to drive home, especially when I was far away from them and they had a long journey. I would always ask them to phone me when they got home, hearing the phone ring and their voices on the other end relieved me so much. But there were occasions when they forgot to phone and then I worried and panicked and had to ask the nurses to phone and check they were safely home. They were always sorry they forgot.

When you are in hospital you have to keep a very close eye on your toenails, especially if they start growing inwards as then you will get problems. They will either be very painful or, if you can't feel pain you will get violent spasms, which will let you know you have pain. So keep an eye on your toenails and get them checked by your nurses or carers. I have found that the best way of looking after my toenails is to have the chiropodist visit periodically.

During long periods in hospital you will notice that your skin and scalp gets very dry and flaky. Your scalp could get severe dandruff very similar to cradle cap. If you cannot move your arms, like myself, it does get very aggravating and irritating and I was forever asking the nurses or my family to get me a hot flannel and rub my scalp really hard until it was all out. They would often use a little bit of shampoo preferably the Nizoral shampoo. I would also use a Nizoral cream on my face so that at the end of the day my skin and scalp felt relieved. If the dandruff was very thick I would ask one of the nurse whom I trusted, to shave my hair off with my hair clippers. Afterwards it felt wonderful. I would be forever praising them for doing it.

One day I was told by the nurses that we would be having a load of Japanese students coming round to look at the place to see how a spinal unit in England is run. I was sitting on the bedpan when a whole crowd of these students waltzed through the ward. They all had cameras and they looked straight at me and said "Ah look!" They then came straight over to me and started to take photos of me! I was wondering what was going on – I thought I was a celebrity! I asked one of the translators with them, "Why are they so fascinated with me that they are taking photo's?" The translator told me that they had never seen a man with red hair before! Great, so that means come tomorrow morning my face will be all over the Japanese press with me sitting on a bedpan! The translator started laughing and translated for the students who then joined in. I made a few more friends that day.

For a short period a foreign exchange student from Japan worked on the ward and I told her all about this incident and she thought it very funny too. Her name is Eri, she is a lovely girl and very thoughtful.

I met a couple of friends in hospital, one called Tom Graham who still writes to me now. He always used to come and see me every day and see how I was getting on, he was actually doing very well with his rehab because he managed to go from his chair to his feet and now he is walking with a stick. I also made another friend called Rob and the same thing happened to him too. He has now got a walking stick. He would still visit me after he left the hospital, as he lived not very far away. I have tried to get in contact with him and for some reason I have lost his address, but one day I will get in touch again somehow.

During my stay there was a young lad called Steven, he was a handicapped boy and had a twin brother called Matthew who was also handicapped. Steven grew very fond of me and came to see me very often, even with his parents. On some occasions he would sneak off without someone seeing him and would come to see me and say, "Breathe Carl, breathe." Sometimes he would grab my locker and throw everything off it, wheel himself up to me and pull my vent tube off. He couldn't understand that I needed the ventilator to breathe. Everyone tried to explain it to him but he just couldn't understand. In the end the nurses had to ban him from coming into the ward. He remembered when people came to his brother and removed the ventilator and how he had eventually learnt to breathe. He couldn't understand that it wouldn't work for me. Gradually Steven learnt to walk. The twins had another brother David and lovely parents who also used to visit and play jokes on me. They used to tease me and ask, "How's your room coming on – have you got those bunk beds ready for Steven and Matthew?" We used to laugh.

For some reason Steven used to pick up words I often said to Gordon the auxiliary nurse – I used to call him a Muppet and I used to say quite a lot, "Bad luck number 12 mate", as number 12 was my unlucky number. Well, Steve would come into the ward saying "Twelve, twelve, bad luck Carl, or Muppet". Gordon would tell him to keep on repeating it, saying it louder and louder and to stomp his feet. It would drive everyone barmy! He used to come backward and forwards saying this all day even though they had banned him from the ward. I must admit I still couldn't help laughing because of the things he did. Many people didn't find Steven funny and used to tell him where to go and get on his way. I suppose that was why he liked me and always came to see me because I never did tell him off at all. One other thing that I do remember about Steven is that one day he came into the ward, threw my jug of water all over the floor and got pushed out of the ward. Later he came back, the nurses were behind the curtains with a patient and my vent came off all by itself! He realised something was wrong and shouted out for the nurses "Nurse, quick Carl can't breathe!" he was racing down the ward but the nurses were not far away. I think that Steven did eventually realise the dangers in coming off of the vent for someone like me.

One morning I was asleep in bed and I heard this really loud screaming coming from the other end of the ward. It frightened the living daylights out of me. I asked to be sat up and said; "What the hell is that!" It was a man playing the bagpipes for St. Andrews Day. I shouted, "Shut up I'm trying to get some sleep here!" Still playing he approached me laughing, so I introduced myself and we had a bit of a laugh. He put his beret on my head and sat with me for a while. One of the nurses took a photograph and as he went on round the ward I told him to make sure he didn't get the pipes stuck up his skirt as he was wearing his kilt. Off he went with a smile and a giggle.

Not long after that incident I was talking to this lovely polite and attractive lady for a while, you know the usual chitchat, how was I etc, and after some time she wandered off to visit with the other patients. I asked the nurse who she was, she was amazed that I hadn't recognised her, "Don't you know?" Well since I had asked it was obvious I didn't! She then told me that it was Cherie Blair, the Prime Minister's wife. Just as she was about to leave my ward I called out "I know who you are now – how's Tony?" She smiled and continued on her way.

While I was at Stoke Mandeville I used to see Sir Jimmy Saville on his travels round the ward visiting the patients. Every time he saw me he used to say "Ahh, my friend, now then my friend, the Smiler." This was because I always used to smile when I saw him. He was mostly with a couple of friends or his minders and occasionally by himself. He would say to people, "When I count to three I'll turn round and give you a really big smile." I used to give him a big smile and couldn't help laughing, as he is a really funny man. One day I asked him where my "Jim'll fix it Badge" was as I was a great admirer of that show and he told me that I should think up something for him to fix. A few days later he came into the ward and wanted to know if I had decided on something he could fix for me. "I don't know Jim, can't think mate" I said, and he told me to give him the biggest smile EVER! So I gave him the biggest smile I could and now I am the proud owner of a very special Jim'll fix it Badge and sticker. I was absolutely delighted and felt very privileged, he went on down the ward humming and whistling as he always did.

One day in August 1999 I was told after my ablutions and dressing to get into my chair quite early as there was someone coming to see me. I hadn't been expecting visitors, so I sat waiting patiently. Sometime later this man walked in with a woman. I could tell that they had stopped in the doorway and were smiling, but I still couldn't tell who it was, as my eyesight was not too good. "Who is it?" A voice replied "What do you mean, who is it?" As soon as I heard his voice I knew straight away who it was! It was my favourite actor, David Jason! I shouted out "Del Boy!" and as he approached me saying, "Hello, how are you then?" I was so overjoyed that I had tears in my eyes. He sat down beside me and introduced his girlfriend Gill. Del Boy asked where they could get a drink and I asked Gordon the Health Care Assistant, to get us all a coffee.

I had photos taken by the sister of the ward who had arranged the visit. David sat with me chatting for quite a while; we talked about his videos covering all of his series. I remember on one of the videos where he said to Rodney and Mickey Pearce, when they were down at the auction after they had bought some lawnmower engines "This stuff is a load of old rubbish". They replied that these were not just ordinary lawnmower engines. Del Boy said, "No, they're a load of broken lawnmower engines!" So when David asked me about my ventilator I told him "'Ere Del, it's not an ordinary ventilator – it's a broken ventilator." We all had a jolly good laugh. David & Gill stayed with me for quite a while, we talked about the actors he worked with and what they were like in real life.

David told me that he would keep in touch with me and that he would have to be going, but before they left Gill told me how she had been trying to get him to marry her! I found her a wonderful and charming lady, and very attractive.

Before these very special visitors left, Del Boy gave me one of his books and a video, which he autographed "To my best fan ever, lots of love David Jason, Luvely Jubbly."

As they were leaving I called out "Del Boy, you're a plonker!" and he called back "Dipstick!"

When they had left I burst into tears. I had so enjoyed their visit and was so very happy.

When I told my family they couldn't believe it, and we decided to tell everyone out there how wonderful David is and how he made my day by contacting the newspapers. All the newspapers caught on to this story and I was in newspapers on a regular basis after that. They wrote about my family and how to raise money for me so that I could buy a special computer, as I so wanted to write a book and get it published. I have also been on the News, and my mum was planning to go on the Trisha Show so that she could tell everyone about how she wanted to raise money for my computer. I also wanted to design business cards. The next time Jimmy Saville came into the hospital he remarked on the fact that every time he read a newspaper it was full of stories about me!

I noticed from the newspaper photos that I was putting on quite a bit of weight so I decided to go on a diet using "Slim Fast" milk drinks. The dietician wasn't very keen on the idea, but I insisted. So, I now have one milkshake for breakfast and one for lunch and a proper meal with fruit in the evening and I have so far managed to loose two stone, which pleases me. Especially as I can't move! I was determined to do it, and I also wanted to make life easier for the carers when they lifted me in and out of bed.

Just before my birthday in October David Jason visited me again and I just couldn't believe it! He had kept his promise and even though he couldn't stay very long I was delighted to see both him and Gill. Again the family told the newspaper and again there were more pictures and interviews. This time they wanted copies of the pictures with Del Boy – I was becoming quite famous!

The food in Stoke Mandeville wasn't much to talk about and at one stage they even closed the canteen down. Quite regularly I used to buy takeaways when finances allowed, but as a result of this I started to put on weight again! I had to be careful. The food in hospital was actually brought in from the main canteen because they closed the "Spinal Canteen" due to lack of money. Jimmy Saville was fighting to re-open it. The food came from Wales and was then cooked on the premises in the main kitchen. Even though I ate the food it was not a pleasant experience for my fellow patients or for me.

The dietician at Stoke Mandeville gave "Slim Fast" a ring to see if I could get them cheaper or even free, as my income was very little. "Slim Fast" agreed to send me a crate of 60 ready-made cans. They then heard that I did really well, so they sent me a further crate. I was really pleased, especially with the fact that I was still loosing the weight and "Slim Fast" helping me to keep my weight down overwhelmed me. They sent me a Christmas card and all the employees signed it. They have been very good to me and I will continue to use their milk shakes.

When you are in a wheelchair and cannot move it is advisable to wear the kind of clothing that is comfortable, make sure that it is quite baggy and not too tight. Also make sure there are no zips or buttons at the back. As spinal injury patients cannot feel, they would not know if anything was digging into their skin and they could mark easily and this could result in pressure sores. I have known some patients to get a warning if they are sitting on something sharp or hard. This warning is something I have mentioned before "Autonomic Dysreflexia," and they will know that something is hurting somewhere. Luckily enough I can still feel, but I still have to make sure there are no buttons or anything else, even creases which will make me feel uncomfortable. This applies to pressure relief too; I don't get that often as I can shuffle my bum about to relieve areas, which is very useful.

When I am in bed and get positioned I prefer to use a 'T' bar. This is a foam pillow in the shape of a 'T', which goes under my knees, and the middle section goes between my legs quite close to the groin so that my legs are in a bent position; almost like sitting in a chair but more elevated. This is very useful as it keeps the legs bent as spasms can occur when your legs are straight. While in this position I also use a rolled duvet at the foot of the bed with two pillows behind so that my feet can rest against it, this is very comfortable. I also have pillows for each arm and hand splints, which are called, paddle splints. These paddle splints are made by the Occupational Therapist and are designed to keep the hand stretched out and in a position where they are maintained and are comfortable. The paddles are made by heating the hard material in the splints in hot water and then moulded into shape on your hand and gradually they get very hard. Your hands can then be placed into the splints and held in place with Velcro straps. Some people may require extra padding around the splint to cushion sensitive areas. These sensitive areas are found when the splints are worn for a while each day to build up the skin tolerance. They normally start off by leaving them on for about an hour, then checking to see if the skin is fine, then leaving them on for a while longer until you can wear them all the time. This applies to leg splints as well.

I also have a head roll, which is positioned under the left side of my head pillow to hold my head over, as my head pulls to the left due to a large spasm in my left shoulder.

The Occupational Therapist helps you to find the correct and most comfortable wheelchair. I have tried many but the one that I am happy with and which I find most comfortable is the Gillingham Tilt. This wheelchair can be reclined and tilted as I get the feeling that I am falling forward, which is very uncomfortable. I also have an adapted armrest, which is totally flat and is designed for my left arm, which doesn't bend very well. The right arm is quite normal and sits in the rest quite nicely. My headrest is also adapted with a little wall on the left-hand side with soft padding to help hold my head over because it pulls to the left. The same applies to my head roll, which I use in bed under the side of the pillow. My chair also has a long tray at the base for my ventilator to sit on when I go out. I also have a standard car battery, which can last on full charge up to about 20 hours. When you have finished with the chair and the ventilator, the battery goes on charge overnight so that it is fully charged for the following day. This idea is excellent for going out and about and is positioned ready on the tray so that it doesn't move about while being pushed along.

The cushion I use is called a Jay 2, which has several layers of gel in the cushion. It is covered by a cushion cover and positioned onto the wheelchair with Velcro so that it doesn't move about. I find this cushion very comfortable. Most people when trying out a cushion suitable for them will go to a seating clinic. This is a special cushion with probes on it that can detect all your pressure areas, the ones that are most vulnerable.

Whilst they are trying out various cushions, a lot of people seem to use a Roho cushion. This is a rubber cushion with several balloon type pockets, which have air in them. This type of cushion is very comfortable whilst you are trying to find the right cushion for you. The Roho can also be used when trying to find the right mattress for your bed.

The mattress that I use is called a Contoura. The bed that I have used and that I am happy with is an electric bed, which has head up and down, tilt down and raise the bed up or down facilities. There are several models of this particular bed but the one that I have used in the past is called an Eggerton. The bed I have now is very similar. Some of these beds are fitted with cot sides to stop people from falling out of bed but I do not use them as I rarely have that kind of problem. The bed also has a footboard with the base and some of them have a headboard too, but I prefer to go without the headboard so that it enables me to go right up the bed.

PHYSIOTHERAPIST - Continued

Whilst in hospital I have seen physiotherapists quite regularly and have benefited from regular body stretches. The physiotherapist will decide how much physio you need and how often. They will assess all your joints and bone structure and move all parts of your body to relieve tightness and to maintain range. The physiotherapist may give you a programme which may consist of one day leg movements or one day arm movements or one day standing or maybe all at once. The physiotherapist is very good at maintaining your movement and the range and will guide you on what they think is best for you.

At one point I was advised by a physiotherapist to have an injection call boxalin, for short they call it box tox. I had this done in my left shoulder to ease the tightness and some of the spasm but I didn't find that it really worked on me. This injection is injected near the muscle and is only done by qualified parties. A similar thing that I had was a Baclofen injection, which was injected into my spinal cord. This actually worked quite well and did relieve the spasm. They do a test to see if you qualify for a Baclafen pump, which is positioned in the base of your stomach and wired up to your spine. This is done in theatre. In the pit of your stomach they insert a little tube, which is topped up with Baclafen. I did not fancy this at all so I carried on with antispasmodic tablets. I have Dantrolene, which is another form of antispasmodic medication.

The physiotherapist is also there for chest physio because a lot of ventilated patients or patients with a trache, experience a lot of secretions building up on their chest. The physiotherapist will help to loosen the secretions by shaking the chest, or percussion or cupping. Sometimes before these chest movements are done, a towel is initially placed on the chest so that the physiotherapist can gently slap or shake the chest without bruising it. Some people like hard shakes some like gentle. I prefer quite a vigorous shake as my secretions can be quite thick and I need a harder shake. I do prefer this. Chest physio can be done at set times by the physio or as required. Some patients need chest physio more than others depending on how bad their chest is. If it becomes really productive on a regular basis they may send off a specimen of sputum to see if it might be infected. If so they may decide to give you a course of antibiotics, which should help clear the chest infection.

A lot of spinal injury patients cannot maintain their body temperature and they tend to take on the temperature around them. So extra thick warm clothing is advised especially when going out or after having a shower as the body temperature drops dramatically and is very hard to get back up without warm clothing or a heated room. If you find that your temperature is not increasing then you may find that you have to use something called a huggy bear. This is placed beneath your sheet or duvet and has hot air pumping through it to help bring up your temperature. You can also use a space blanket, which is a large blanket made of foil which is placed on your body under your sheet or duvet. I must say that I have used both at the same time. I do know that some people can tell if you have hypothermia or are very cold as you may have very pale skin and be cold to the touch, blue lips and a temperature of around 34°-35°, whereas a normal temperature is around about 36°-37°. If your temperature goes over 37° you may decide to take off a lot of your top covers or the space blanket or the huggy bear. This should then bring down the temperature – if not there may be other problems or complications, but normally if I do get hot I would open a window or put a fan on me until I feel cool enough and my temperature goes down. If I can't tell how cool I am then I would go back and use a thermometer, which is a good guideline.

The thermometer is a glass rod with mercury in it and a temperature dial normally starting from the lower 30° to 40°. The thermometer can be placed under your tongue, in the armpit or groin area. These are the warmest parts of your body and can detect a good temperature. You can also use something called a tymphanic thermometer, which is a little machine similar to a small gun, which has a probe at the end of it covered by a plastic cap, which is placed in your ear. It has a little button, which is pushed and automatically displays your temperature on a digital screen. I personally think this piece of equipment is very effective and accurate and I prefer it. You may decide to have your blood pressure taken quite regularly, this can be done by using a blood pressure machine and a stethoscope. They find the blood pressure by feeling the pulse and listening when the cuff of the machine is inflated, they listen for the sound of the pulse to stop. This is the high reading. The cuff is then deflated and they listen for the sound of the pulse coming back – this is the lower reading. There is also an automatic blood pressure machine, which takes B/P readings and puts the result on to a screen. A normal blood pressure reading is 130/70 but this varies from patient to patient. If the BP is too high they have to rectify the problem. Sometimes pain will cause a rise in blood pressure and drugs will be administered to reduce pain and then the BP will lower. If the BP is too low intravenous fluids may be given.

There was an occasion when I decided to use herbal medicine. This consisted of remedies such as Lobelia, Hawthorn, Barbary and Camomile capsules, herbal clay and a herbal drink called Super Food. These were all mixed up, apart from the clay, with orange juice. All these remedies were to help different areas of the body but I found them all very expensive. I really don't know if they worked or not, but they did not harm me at all and it was a good experience. The clay was mixed with olive oil and was supposed to remove pus from wounds or injured areas. I tried this on the back of my neck where I had had my stroke and where we found a discharge. I don't know if the clay did help but there again it did not harm me in any way. In the end I returned to my normal tablets, as I could not keep up the herbal remedies because of the cost.

I have also seen a few faith healers and they guide you in different directions and use different charms for areas of the body, such as coloured ribbons or charms.. Yet again, I really don't know if this was any good or not, but I gave it a try and you never know until you find out about these things. One of the faith healers did actually ask to feel a possession of mine. So, one of my brothers decided to give him a chain that I used to wear round my neck. Apparently she held this chain and saw my bedroom. She described it to my brother but what made me laugh was one thing she said about my curtains, as I did not have any! She actually said, "I see a room with no curtains" – that did make me laugh as I thought to myself "Blimey, what else can she see in my room – can't I get any privacy!"

There was another faith healer who said he could see me in a wheelchair, but he said I was going to be alright.

MEDICATION

Ever since my time in hospital I have been on mainly the same medication, but there were times when a few of them did vary. I now seem to have found the most suitable medication for me, these are: -

- Nortriptyline 100mg at night for relaxation and depression
- Lamotrigine 25mg at night for seizures

At one time I was on Tegretol for seizures but this was changed as it was expensive. I was also having night sedation initially.

- Diazapam for the first 3 months then
- Temezepan up until 8 months ago.
- Baclofen for my spasms at one time
- Dantrolene 50mgs 3 times a day for muscle spasms
- Domperidone at breakfast and lunchtime 10mg to prevent nausea and vomiting.
- Lactulose and Sennakot to prevent constipation - taken at teatime.
- Glycerine suppositories in the morning for bowel action.

Previously I was also having Microlax and Phosphate enemas and on occasions Dolcolax Suppositories, thankfully now I only need glycerine!

- Terbutaline nebuliser 5mgs 3 times a day
- Saline nebuliser when required
- Saline directly into trachea tube
- Paracetamol 1gm every night for pain relief and as required during the day.

I have also initially been taking Diclofenic Sodium – a stronger painkiller, which is a non-steroidal anti-inflammatory drug. Thankfully now I no longer have such severe violent pounding headaches. Also in the early days I had severe neuralgia caused by my stroke. I also had a facial twitch.

HOSPITAL RADIO

Whilst I was in Stoke Mandeville they opened up a hospital radio station called Stoke Mandeville Hospital Radio. In the beginning you could only pick the station up on the small portable radios issued to the patients, but it eventually went out on 157 waves on normal radio. I gradually got to know all the radio team because they used to come round and ask all the patients if they would like a request on the radio. I became their best customer! I would give them a list of requests and they would play them and always mentioned my name. They were all volunteers. I always used to listen to my requests and they would say ' We've been to see Carl again and have a list of requests to play!' They also mentioned my fund raising appeals and would record my favourite songs for me to play on my tape player.

They would also mention when David Jason visited or any articles about me that appeared in the newspaper. Eventually they came round less frequently due to visiting other wards. Before I left Stoke Mandeville they gave me a card and wished me good luck. At one time they did invite me to go on their radio show but I didn't get around to it because I came down with a chest infection and MRSA but, I would liked to have visited them to see how it was all run. I do hope they still think of me.

LEAVING STOKE MANDEVILLE

I had been at Stoke Mandeville for about a year when they started looking at alternative accommodation for me. I visited several interim places, one was called the Aspen Unit, another one was called the Holy Cross in Hazlemere, also Treetops in Colchester. I visited them all but was not so keen on the Holy Cross or the Aspen Unit as it was so far away from my family and I would only get a visit perhaps once a week. Treetops I did like but, at the time I was in-between social workers – one would say, "Yes, you're going," and the other would say "No you're not," and in the end they gave up! Then I was back to square one. When I started appearing in the newspapers Beckingham Court saw me and got in contact with me. They were interested in me! I agreed to go and visit, they showed me the room I would be in and explained about the care I would have, I was quite impressed as it was a double room.

In the end I agreed, and their carers gradually came to Stoke Mandeville for training, this went on for several weeks as well as the training continuing at Beckingham Court. When it was all agreed they made arrangements to start adapting the room. The ceiling hoist and shower room was installed, a shower trolley was provided for me to lie on. My bed, suction machine and all necessary equipment for my care package was sorted. This was all funded by Social Services and Juliette Ashton and Anne Morris were in charge of my funding. They have been the best couple that I have had on my side in charge of funding since I have been in hospital. I have had several social workers that I have found useless – giving out promises that they didn't keep. I was promised a four-bedroom bungalow in the Prettygate area of Colchester. The Community Occupational Therapist did all the plans to scale on how it would be adapted for my needs, but it all fell through.

I felt very happy with Ann and Juliette and intended to keep them on my side. They also provided and paid for additional training with the Brownsville, which is a spinal injury-training centre. They arranged to be in charge for most of the training, but I was going to have a lady called Mandy Arkle who used to be a sister on my ward at Stoke Mandeville – she left Stoke Mandeville to work for Brownsville she was going to be in charge of my carers training, but she left and I was appointed a lady called Pauline Robinson. I found her work very thorough and to the point. She actually told me that I was her best client. She told me that I actually got up every day – did my entire physio, ablutions etc. She told me that a lot of her clients didn't do any of that but lay in bed all day covered in pressure sores and didn't worry about their care. When she told me that I was her best client I felt very privileged. I do not intend to let myself go downhill in any way. I am very particular about my care, and about who looks after me, and the quality of my care. I am very verbally independent in instructing my carers about the care they deliver and demand a high standard.

A lot of my equipment, clothing and personal belongings were gradually brought from Stoke Mandeville by my family. I was left with only the bare essentials, which came with me in the Paravan. I came down with Fred, Dr. Raj and a member of my family. That morning before I left I said my farewells and good riddance to the staff. A few of them brought me gifts and farewell cards and I did say that I would keep in touch. When I arrived at Beckingham Court all my equipment was ready for me, wardrobe, suction, vent, tilt table, etc. etc. Alison Rich, the nurse manager, several of the staff and Juliette Ashton greeted me too. I was so overwhelmed to be out of hospital and basically back to normality – back in the community. The day I moved in there was a welcome party. Fred and the Doctor stayed for a little while to settle me in but I was on a high all day and didn't sleep at all that night. I was still on a high several days later. I thoroughly enjoyed having one to one care, I didn't have that at Stoke Mandeville and felt like a king, as I was not used to it. It gradually grew on me and I got used to it. I still did have disagreements but they were all settled eventually.

Being so close to home is something that I cannot explain. I am so pleased to be near all my family and they regularly pop in every day, and at any time. I never believed that I would be so close to them all again, but that first night I came here I did celebrate with champagne and Chinese takeaway. I am gradually getting to know all the staff here. It will take a while to become confident with all of them but I am beginning to know a few of them.

I have had my best friend Dean and his family visit me, they were only able to visit me once at Stoke. One of my other friends called Steve (who we used to nickname Beavis – from Beavis & Butthead) was also mine and Dean's friend. We all used to go out together. I discovered he has emigrated to Australia. I still think about him and it is sad that he is so far away but I think he went out there to better himself – which I don't blame him for and wish him good luck. I would love to see him again as I last saw him during 1998.

Whilst I have been here at Beckingham Court I have had several visits from Juliette who keeps me updated in my care and equipment. She has been very good to me and I intend to keep her but, one thing I am not very happy about is my benefit – it is very little. I am entitled, due to my disability, £37 a week for a vehicle but I am only getting £13 week incapacity benefit as I am in a nursing home. I am not very happy about this. The thing that upsets me is that I still have to provide for toiletries, clothing, T.V. licence and phone bill, which I consider a necessity for someone in my situation, not a luxury. All this has to come out of £13 a week. I am pleased that I now have a very good advocate, Helen Leigh as I have had several advocates who have left the job. I find Helen trustworthy and reliable, she is making enquiries for me in other areas i.e. tax, insurance, MOT for a vehicle which all has to be paid for by someone. She is going to look into local charities as well to see if they can help in any way. My family are also raising money for me and are doing very well.

The first item on my fund raising agenda is a computer, which will be adapted for my use, other items will come later as my fund raising progresses. I am really happy with the fundraising from my family and with my advocate too. I really hope she stays with me.

One thing I do like about Beckingham Court is the physiotherapy I can have whenever I want. There is an appointed physiotherapist here called Gordon who gives me a good stretch whenever I require it. Any other physio I may need comes from the carers so I am rarely without it. Other training in different areas is coming on gradually; I am really comfortable with most of the carers but feel it will be a while before I am fully confident with everyone. You must understand that I rely on the carers for all my needs as I cannot do anything for myself and I must feel confident at all times. This is one of my main concerns, which I have addressed several times. I do understand that on some occasions carers are hard to cover due to annual leave or sickness but I am not asking for much, only the best care that I feel I deserve.

I must say that I think that if I am appointed carers that I don't know or are not comfortable or entirely happy with, I am afraid that the saying goes – make do won't do! I rely on everyone and if I am unhappy then my family are unhappy and it causes all sorts of problems that we don't want. We want everyone to get along, carers and family, we want a good relationship and not any arguments as we all need to have the same aim which is to make me feel happy, safe and secure.

Since I have been here I have found the choice of food excellent – the best that I have ever had in all my stays in hospital. I have a good choice in what I like but I still have my Slim Fast and a meal in the evening of my own choice. Slim Fast heard about my fundraising – The Carl Holmes Appeal – and donated me another crate of Slim Fast cans and also a cheque for £500 towards my computer. I was very pleased with their donation and I intend to thank them as well as other people who have donated to my appeal.

I have been on Slim Fast for about 8 months now and I have managed to loose over 2 stone! I am very pleased especially since I cannot move and am not able to burn the calories off. I am really pleased that I started this and I did it off my own back and stuck to it religiously. I do have one day off a week where I have whatever

I want to eat, I call it my "sin day" and this is on each and every Sunday.

All of my equipment and things like my catheter mount, filters and tubing, trache dressings and conveens have dates for them to be changed, and these are recorded in a folder. Normally the catheter mount is changed on alternate days with the leg bag, suction tubing, suction machine lining and yanker sucker. The HME filter, trache dressing, convene, night drainage bag and saline for tracheostomy are changed daily and the ventilator tubing, irrigation water bag, nebuliser giving set, trache holder tapes are all changed weekly. Other things changed less frequently are the auto feed chamber, which is changed weekly and the filters on the suction and ventilators, blue filter on front of ventilator and the reservoir bag – all monthly. My tracheostomy tubing is changed every 12 weeks at home and every 4 weeks in hospital. The reason why a lot of my things are changed less frequently at home than in the hospital is because there are more germs harbouring in a hospital than there are outside in your own home.

When I'm in bed and getting ready to settle I have special heel type boots called Spencos and these protect my heels from getting red and sore, where in the past they have got a bit red without protection. These work very well for me, but what is quite funny is in the morning when I get ready to deal with all my ablutions my Spenco boots are no longer on my heels! They have worked their way up my leg, which looks quite comical because it looks like I've just come back from a cricket match! Before I used Spencos I used to use the heel pads which are a lot smaller and are universal as they can be used for heels and elbows. I Suppose that you could also use the Spencos on your elbows but I prefer to use the heel pads or elbow pads as some might call it on my right elbow. When I'm in the chair my right elbow does get a bit red.

While I was at Stoke Mandeville I experimented with several devices that can operate things like lights and curtains, T.V. and stereos, basically anything electrical. These can be turned on by using either a little switch in the hand, which I didn't really get on with, or a voice control system, which I am working towards getting for my home, so that I can have a little bit more independence. I have tried out several systems and to me they are very comical because things like curtains open and close on command at about 100mph, and when I saw this I was laughing so much I was in tears! I very much hope I can get one for my home and quite quickly as it will keep me very amused along with everything else I'm doing! The light can also operate on an environmental control, but it's best to have it rigged up to specific lights that you're going to use quite regularly, or you'll be there all day trying to find the light you want on!

Since I have moved out of hospital there have been a few teething problems regarding stock and equipment and things not arriving on a regular basis when they are needed, e.g. things like dressings, tracheostomy tubing etc. Now that everything is all sorted I am receiving regular deliveries but, one thing that did bug me a lot was the conveens. I was given the right name but the wrong make and they kept blowing up and twisting just like a balloon when they were full of urine and either leaking or just exploding. This was very upsetting and uncomfortable. It is quite distressing and it can on some occasions really piss me off if it happens a few times a day. Some people have recommended alternative methods, perhaps catherisation, which is a tube that goes into the penis or another tube that goes straight into the bladder, which is called a supapubic catheter. But, I do not fancy this particular way and I am strongly against this method for someone like myself who can "go" by themselves. I have known some people to use a bottle to pass urine and I have heard that some women can use a femidom, if suitable for them.

While I was at Stoke Mandeville I had a lot of problems with my tracheostomy drying up and blocking off and this happened quite regularly. So what I decided to do and am very happy with, is to try humidification. I started to use this all the time but have gradually been able to wean myself off humidification during the daytime and now I only have it at night. I have found this very comfortable and less distressing to me as I now have fewer blockages. The humidifier that I had in Stoke Mandeville was called a Fischer Paykel and I had the temperature set on 40°. This kept my lungs and secretions quite moist and loose and easy to suction. The humidifier is situated on the base or near the base on a standard drip stand and has a bag of sterile water, with a tube coming out of it going into the humidifier. This is called "a giving set" and delivers the fluid down the tube into the auto feed chamber where it's heated up and then dispensed into steam. It then travels through a blue wet circuit which is connected at one end to the ventilator and goes through the humidifier and then through to the other end which connects onto my trachea. This is used without a filter, just a catheter mount.

When I first arrived at Beckingham Court I had a different kind of humidifier and you could not alter the temperature so it was set on 37.4°c thereabouts, which some people are happy with, but not for me, as I still kept blocking off on regular occasions. I was told that the model I had was no longer in use but I have actually found out that the humidifier that I like is still being made, which I now have and I was able to exchange the newer one which I was given, for the one that I prefer. In the humidifier is a water trap with a water level, which you must not exceed. If the water does exceed this level then all you have to do is take the pot out and empty the excess and put it back again.

The humidifier I had at Stoke Mandeville used water bags and these were getting used at a very quick pace. One bag would roughly last about a day, but the water bags are now lasting me a good 3-4 days or sometimes longer, depending on how often and how long I use the humidifier.

I have got a funny feeling that the humidifier that I had in Stoke Mandeville was burning up way too quickly as we had to change the water bag so frequently. You have to use sterile water for irrigation and I have found out in the past that some people have put up bags of saline instead. This is salt water and when the heat reached the water coming down the salt would then crystallise in the tubing so this is not recommended!

As I am now in a more homely environment I still have daily routines but I can actually do them when it suits me. In a hospital this is not possible and in Beckingham Court where I'm living now I can choose to do my ablutions and physio and get up into my chair when it suits me. But I still do prefer daily routines and set times so that I can organise my days' activities. I usually start my wash around 8.30am. This includes going on the bedpan, doing all of the equipment change, getting dressed and getting positioned correctly in my chair. This normally takes most of the morning but sometimes it can be earlier. During the day I see the physiotherapist Gordon, who gives me a really good stretch and once or twice a week I go on the tilt table. I also get the nurses and carers to do my passive movements, this is very nice indeed and relieves me throughout my entire body and leaves me nice and supple. I also instruct the nurses and carers on how to move my joints and also how to give my chest a good shake to loosen the secretions for suctioning.

Throughout the day, whilst not on the humidifier, I do like two or three mls of saline squirted into my trachea to keep my chest moist and to stop it drying out. I also have saline nebulisers as well. Throughout the day I do things like puzzles, watching videos and going out to restaurants, pubs, cinema and shopping. Articles about me are regularly in the newspapers and they are talking about my book, which I'm in the process of writing and the stationary business that I want to start with my voice activated computer, which will hopefully be funded by the Carl Holmes Fundraising Campaign. In the future I will attend some charity events organised to raise money for me so I can buy a computer and transport, and other necessities, all of which other people take for granted. All the money that has been raised for me is going into a separate account called the Carl Holmes Appeal. I dearly appreciate everyone's' efforts.

I do look forward to my evening meal that I have throughout the week as well as the Slim Fast during the day. I really look forward to Sundays where anything goes, where I do eat what I want but I also moderate it and have smaller meals rather than big feasts which tend to bloat me, so I do take things easy and eat sensibly. Towards the evening if I'm feeling tired then I will ask if I can go back to bed to be made comfortable. During the night I normally stay on my back without pressure relief. The same goes for the chair, because I can feel and I can wriggle about a bit, once I'm comfortable that's me sorted for the day, unless I have a huge spasm and then I'm out of position and I will need sorting out again. But when I'm in bed I either like watching my videos or listening to my music or generally just chatting with the carers. I regularly have plenty of visitors in the evenings, which keeps me busy and occupied.

I'm so glad that I'm now near to my family and friends and that they can pop in whenever they like as my room is treated just like my own home. In hospital I had fewer visitors because of the distance from my family. My room here is lovely and big as it is a 2-bedded room designed for me and I have everything in it that I need. I have my bed, my TV, my video, my hi-fi, wardrobe, drawers, wheelchair, and tilt table and it's all decorated the way I want. I have a door leading out onto the car park and I have a good view because I can see everyone arriving and leaving. I also have a little en-suite toilet for the carers and visitors. My carer naturally uses this toilet for emptying my leg bag and bedpan.

I also have my own shower trolley and portable suction units, which I use for the shower room and when I go out. My shower room is down the corridor and I shower once or twice a week. It requires two carers to shower and turn me and to dry me. Two people shower me, and the third person "bags me" with the ambu bag, this means we don't have to take the whole ventilator with us. The shower room also has a fitted heater, which needs turning on about half an hour before to heat up the room for me. When I'm being dried the conveen is then put on me and connected back up to the night bag, but on some occasions I do have to use granuflex or a cold gel called "second skin" which protects red areas around the penis which I sometimes get. After I've been dried thoroughly I'm transferred back onto the bed and wrapped up in my sheet and duvet for me to warm up otherwise I could become hypothermic. Once I have warmed up I can then be transferred onto my tilt table or into my wheelchair.

The shower trolley that I use here is slightly shorter than the one that I used at Stoke Mandeville, but I prefer this because I cannot spasm down the trolley whilst being showered. The tilt table that I use is positioned by the bed so I can slide on, then I am strapped down to hold me in position and I am raised to a standing position or to a height I am happy with. This is very similar to a standing bed, which I have tried but didn't like, as the position didn't feel very comfortable and also it didn't tilt. It also had cot sides, which I do not like because in the past I have banged my legs and feet on them when I have spasmed. The tilt table I use also has a footboard for my feet to rest on so that when I am raised up I actually feel as though I am standing. This is very good for spasms and blood pressure, but sometimes for some people, if they are raised up too quickly, they can pass out as their blood pressure can drop, but I cannot say I have ever had that experience and thank God for that!

I am then transferred on a daily basis into my chair and made comfortable in a similar way as being made comfortable in my bed. I must not have any creases and I must be positioned in the proper way, this means being right back in my chair and dead straight. I don't like looking as if my legs are swaying to the side. If this happens I tend to make a joke out of it and I say I am going to try slaloming on the ski slope, because this is what it resembles and this does make everybody laugh.

Whilst I have been in Beckingham Court it has taken me quite a long time to remember everyone's names and their capabilities. I have been through this before when I moved from hospital to hospital but I did meet several nurses in hospital that I didn't get along with! Some were quite rude and horrible, but since I have been here I can rarely say I have come across this problem with the regular staff. I have come across a few problems with the "bank staff," which I have reported and they are no longer dealing with my care.

I have mentioned before that I suffer with short-term memory loss and since I have been at Beckingham Court I have kept records of all my daily events, phone calls and visitors so that if I do forget all I have to do is to refer to my dairy where I have documented it all. My family and social worker thought up this idea and I think it is excellent therapy for my memory as well as a very good idea. I wish that I had done this in the past because I did have regular things that I had to remember, as well as learning verbal independence, so this would have been very useful to me. I don't believe that I could do without my diary now that I have one.

Whilst I have been at Beckingham Court my family have been organising a lot of charity events, and I have several coming up in the future. But they are also going to write to companies and superstores to see if they can donate anything that could be useful to me, such as toiletries, clothing, entertainment etc., as my income in the nursing home is very little – hardly worth mentioning! My family have approached the Co-op electrical store and they have gladly donated me a television with ceefax. I was so overwhelmed that we put a bit in the newspaper and said how generous a lot of people had been with donations with both money and gifts for my use. Whenever anyone does donate something we do thank them by putting it in the newspaper. I do have a good amount of money donated to me in the Carl Holmes Appeal, which is still going on and will be left open for other donations and charity fund raising events on my behalf in the future. Everyone is doing lots of charitable events for me and I also have a lot coming up in the future which I am going to attend. I have had a good amount of help from Slim Fast with donations of drinks as well as a cheque for £500. I have had a lot of response from people since I have been in the papers, as well as letters from my good friend David Jason, who I have been told wants to do something to help me.

My family are doing ever so well at all this fund raising and are dedicated to it. They are hoping in the near future to organise a massive tombola where all the money raised will be donated to my appeal. They are going to try to ask a good selection of shops if they would donate something towards the tombola. Everybody that has helped me, or is going to help me, will get mentioned in the newspaper when my appeal is near the end or whenever I am mentioned in the newspaper!

I do on a regular basis, think about what is going to happen in the future, good or bad I do try to get on with my life as much as I can. My future plan for myself is for me to get out as much as I can, as regularly as possible, and to pack my life with daily activities and events.

I do want to make myself well known so that not only are people aware of me, but also aware of others in a similar situation. I am working towards getting my own vehicle, which I intend to use quite regularly to enable me to pursue my daily outings and events and to also attend charitable events. I would also, in the near future, love to give out any information that may help people in a similar condition to myself. I do intend to start up my own stationary business, as well as writing a book on my computer, so that I can design business cards and birthday cards for people. I also intend to keep in contact with all the friends I have made whilst being in hospital, as well as some of the staff that I get along with.

After being in Beckingham Court for six weeks I had an out-patients appointment at Stoke Mandeville which I attended by ambulance in my wheelchair. I was there a number of hours and they did a lot of check-ups on me, such as blood tests, x-rays, etc and they asked how I was coping and getting on. I also had an ultrasound on my kidneys and they found a couple of kidney stones, which had got slightly bigger. After the ultrasound the Consultant that I am under, a Mr. Gardener, came and explained to me that I should consider having them removed, but the choice was mine. I did ask him about the risks involved in having the operation and the problems if I did not. I did have a bit of a cry as I was quite shocked and didn't expect that I would have to go back into hospital again. He did tell me there are several ways in which kidney stones can be removed, either by surgery or blasting them out! They sit you in a tub of water and blast them with a type of laser and I do believe there are other ways around this but I have not been given the full details yet until they find out how big the stones are. Then they will either admit me back into hospital or I will have to attend an appointment where they can remove the stones on the same day. So I will either be going to have it done and come home the same day or the next, whichever I would prefer. I gave some urine samples so that the specialist can monitor my kidney function.

Throughout my stay the staff have had additional training from a lady called Pauline who works for Brownville Associates, which is a care-training agency, who set up care packages. Pauline has done quite a bit of intensive training and is going to continue within the home and also with future help from Brownville's. Whenever Pauline is not here there is training going on in the room upstairs where they have all the equipment and dummies required for training. I have been very impressed with Pauline's work and I hope that she will continue the training for a while. I first met her in Stoke Mandeville when she came to introduce herself to me and I thought to myself she seems the one for the job. She was telling me that in the hospital a lot of the equipment and things like tubing, catheter mounts, leg bags etc are changed quite frequently due to bugs and germs and infections.

Now that I am in the community, equipment like that mentioned can be changed less frequently as there are fewer bugs in your own home, unlike hospitals. I personally think that disposable equipment should be changed frequently as bugs can harbour anywhere. I did have a little laugh about it as I said does that means the bugs say to themselves, "Oh no, this is not a hospital, we won't fester here then!" My personal opinion is that a germ is a germ and there is no restriction on where a germ will go. This is my personal opinion. I am very impressed with all Pauline's work and I am very glad that she is going to continue with the training.

When you are outside in the community you an entitled to a mobility allowance, this is money towards a vehicle. When I came to Beckingham Court I was told that there was a three-year waiting list for getting a vehicle, so I did say, "Well how do you expect me to travel about then?" I was then told I had to use taxi vans, which are taxis, which allow the seats to come out in the back of the van and allow your wheelchair to be lifted into the taxi using either a ramp or an hydraulic lift. The wheelchair is then fastened down by several buckles and seat belts secured to the ground. These secure the chair in a safe position when the vehicle is in motion. For someone like myself I couldn't wait for three years to get my own vehicle and have to rely on taxis. So what my family and I have done is we have bought a second hand one which used to belong to Broomfield Hospital in Chelmsford. This ambulance is very similar to the van or taxi van I have used before at Stoke Mandeville. The van is in excellent condition throughout and I am very pleased with it. Luckily enough we found out about this van from the ambulance men who transferred me from Stoke Mandeville to Beckingham Court, so that was a bit of good luck really, and as the saying goes it's not what you know, it's who you know! The van has been thoroughly checked out by Toby my brother who is a mechanic and he has told me that I couldn't have got a better deal.

Since I have been in Beckingham Court I have found the food excellent, better than most restaurants that I have been to. The quality of the food here has no comparison to the food in hospitals. I have a good relationship with the kitchen staff and I am allowed to have basically whatever I want, which is very tempting, but I am still sticking to my Slim Fast, which I intend to do for quite a while yet.

I cannot believe how thoroughly clean everything is, for example, all my linen and the room itself and bathroom, are cleaned thoroughly on a daily basis, including all towels and flannels, which I am overwhelmed by, as I am very particular about cleanliness.

When I was in the hospital I had regular visits from a Chiropodist, who comes out to see how your feet and toenails are, and they tell you if you need treatment. They maintain the toenails to make sure they are not growing inwards and see if your have any dry skin or broken areas. Now that I am in the community, the Chiropodist's visits are less frequent so I have devised my own nail care kit which allows the carers to keep on top of my nail growth until I can be allocated a Chiropodist. My nails cause me terrible pain if they get too long and then also cause me to spasm on a regular basis

I regularly get very dry skin on my scalp and face due to the dry atmosphere within the hospital and home. To keep the dry skin at bay I regularly use a special face cream and shampoo called Nizoral. This relieves all dry skin and also the soreness that often arises over a period of time. Sometimes my scalp can be so dry and flaky that the best thing that I have found is to shave all my hair off with the hair clippers that I bought a couple of years ago. This works wonders for me and I have had it all shaved off on the shortest grade, a number one. The hospitals do have their own hairdressers, but I found this very expensive, especially being on a low income. I have my own clippers, which I use quite regularly and the nurses are happy to do my hair for me.

When I was younger I used to hate the colour of my hair as it was very bright, like an orange! Quite often, especially when I was young and at school, people would continually make fun of it and tease me. So, as I was growing up I decided to highlight it to a blonde colour, which everyone seemed to like, including me.

When I had my stroke they shaved off all my hair for the first time. I couldn't believe how the colour and style suited me, especially with the fact the colour had got darker over a period of time and now I love it and would not get rid of it. I do wish that I had had this colour earlier on!

When I was younger and went out quite regularly, I seemed to suffer with paranoia. I felt that everybody was looking at me! I suppose in a way this was a reflection on my childhood. I did try to avoid certain activities at school such as swimming and sports, due to my feeling of being watched. But since my accident it does still sometimes come out due to my disability, but I don't always feel like this. I have had regular counselling, but I feel that the only way through it is to get through it by yourself. Before my accident I used to argue with my family quite regularly for no reason and everyone seemed to come and go and take everyday activities for granted, but now I have this disability, it has brought my family and me very close indeed. There are occasionally slight arguments, but not like before. The arguments have often arisen during my stay in hospital and we have had several problems along the way in getting what we want and what is essential for my care and rehabilitation. Arguments have been brought on by some inadequate care and equipment, which is still ongoing, but you will get problems along the way, which I have found with quite a number of people that I have spoken to who have been in a similar situation. The only way to sort out problems is to confront them as they come along. This is what my family and I do, the saying goes that you do have to fight to get what you want and it's not an easy battle. Quite often there are tears and remorse along the way, but we all think that as the problems are sorted out and not left, then the relationship with everyone is much easier.

While I was in Stoke Mandeville I learnt about an environmental control system, which operates things like lights, TV and videos, c.d. players, anything that operates from an electric switch or a remote control. I found this system quite amusing as there are several types on the market, some are voice activated and some are operated by buttons or a switch or even a little pad which is placed on any part of your body which has movement. This pad has a probe attached to it so when you move a specific part of your body, the probe detects this movement and activates anything that is programmed into it. The one I have seen has a voice box, which actually spoke out a menu of things that were programmed into it. The one I saw would say "Curtains, lights, doorbell, TV. Hi-fi," and I would press a switch when I wanted to select the required command. I found the switch very difficult to work so I would find a voice-activated system very useful as I have quite a clear voice. I much admire the system I saw on a demonstration film and I also saw one on the famous Alfred Hitchcock film 'The Bedroom Window,' played by Christopher Reeve. I found his system very useful and entertaining. I do very much hope that I will get a similar system in the near future.

Throughout my stay in hospital I have met a lot of people, some staff, some patients and I have had a lot of promises from people to help me to raise money in order to buy the things I need. Some of them said they would do sponsorships and others said that they would write to different companies and charities to see what they would donate. Naturally I was excited when they offered to help me, but some of it never materialised and it just seemed that people were making false promises. But other times I did believe them as I thought they were genuinely trying to help me, because they were all telling me how well they had achieved things and got what they wanted from all different charities. So many of them told me how they went about it and how easy it was to get. In the end, my family decided that they are going to raise the money by advertising me in the newspapers, and saying how they are trying to raise money for me, and asking if anybody could help me to buy the things that I need.

This has gone on for quite a while and I am still appearing in newspapers on a regular basis and have an appeal going which was set up by Essex County Standard and seems to be catching on everywhere else. There is quite a bit of money in my appeal already and still it goes on. I have also been in the papers regarding donations from superstores like the Co-op, who donated a top of the range Philips TV/video with a good size screen for my eyesight. Everybody who has donated, and any future donations, will be reported to the newspapers as a way of thanking them publicly.

Everything, from my TV, to Slim Fast, and other donations towards my appeal, are gratefully appreciated by my family and me. I'm so pleased that it is going to be an ongoing thing, and I must say that all the newspapers involved have created a lot of publicity for me. And I am sure that everybody who donated must also appreciate the publicity when they are mentioned for their help.

Together, with my family and friends I hope to continue to do this and have several charity events where they would like me to appear, which I will be glad to do.

Since I have been discharged from Stoke Mandeville I have had to build up a lot of trust with the nursing staff at Beckingham Court in all aspect of my care. It is very difficult learning everybody's names, but this has happened wherever I have been in the past few years. Now that I have my own vehicle I feel as though I am more independent with being able to have a choice in where I can go and whenever. But at present it is very difficult to be totally flexible in going out with the staff here because they are not entirely over staffed, and that would leave the rest of the home short. So what I eventually would like, which I think would be best all round, is my own care package, which includes my own carers who are dedicated to me. In other words, independent from the rest of the home. I do hope that this will come about in the very near future, as this is what I have wanted all along. This would give me the chance to get to know them all while I'm in Beckingham Court and I can then decide which ones I like and prefer and which ones I don't.

As I am in Beckingham Court for at least a year I can decide on whether or not I would like to stay here. If I left Beckingham Court I should then get as promised my own home in the community, with the carers that I have chosen. I can only do this if I get my own carers and I would like to get this underway as soon as possible. I have told numerous people, including my family, what I prefer and living in my own home with my own care team is it. Living in Beckingham Court is a good experience for me all round as I am basically getting the idea what it is like out of hospital and living in the community. I also think that being in Beckingham Court is a good experience for the nurses, as they can get an idea in what it is like looking after young disabled people like myself. They can then decide if they would like to venture down this avenue, as I am sure that now many people know that I am here they may decide to come here, if they live within the area. Or the nurses who are looking after them could possibly mention Beckingham Court to other young people, or tell their patients to at least give it a try and see how they get on. Because I think that this is and will be a good interim place for the Essex area, as many of these types of nursing homes are mainly scattered over the rest of the country, as I know myself, because I have visited a lot of them and didn't like the idea of being so far away from my family. I do think that many other families feel like this and may not have been so lucky to have a number of nursing homes so close to where they live.

When I did visit Stoke Mandeville after six weeks of my discharge, I couldn't believe how lucky I was to be out of hospital, and at first I did feel that I would miss being there, but I must admit even the day I left I was just so glad to be out of there. Now that I am out, I don't feel or imagine that I could ever go back into hospital, and basically, I don't ever want to go through that again and I really don't know how I have kept sane through all of this. I have also been told this by other people on numerous occasions, but I have told them, as well as myself, that really you have to keep on top of it, otherwise you do fall to pieces. I must admit that I haven't always been cheerful all along, but I have seen many people are very depressed and upset about their condition and I have seen on many occasions a lot of them being very, very abusive. I must admit, I have very rarely been like this at all because having this kind of temperament is not in me and it doesn't get you anywhere. In fact, it makes things worse between your relationship with the nurses and your condition and causes a bad atmosphere all round. Not only with the nurses but the rest of the patients and the families, as well as your own. I have seen a lot of depressed people in hospital and I do know what they are going through because I have been there myself. I have seen and heard a lot of people that feel as though they are suicidal and want to give up. I have been there myself. But I must tell you, all through my experience that it isn't easy, in fact, it is very difficult, but you have to try to do this for yourself and your family, or you will bring everyone else down with you.

One of the difficult things that I have found with my disability is planning all my daily routines, because doing all of this is very tiring. Things like washing, dressing, getting up and doing physio and other activities. I found it extremely tiring in the early days but you do gradually get yourself into a routine and you get used to it and it gets to be part of your daily life. You cannot do everything all at once. I must admit that not every day you feel motivated to do things, but I rarely have this and I do try to do as much as I can. I have seen many people who are not motivated at all and just don't bother with any daily routines and who are not interested in getting on with their life at all. Some of them just lie in bed all day and don't bother with caring for themselves at all. I mean I have seen so many people that don't bother washing or caring about their skin, or even caring about anybody, they just lie in bed all day and are miserable. Basically, what's the point you might as well pull yourself together and get on with your life, because where is it going to get you. Basically having no motivation will send you to an early grave.

From my own experience, and I know that this applies to others too, it is when you have nurses looking after you that you're not happy with, or you don't like, you're enthusiasm goes straight out of the window! Many a times have I had someone that I don't like or am not happy with and I go all quiet and don't bother talking and I know that this applies to others, because I have actually spoken to them about it, and they have told me exactly the same thing. But, as well as not being happy, you also feel very uncomfortable, cautious and wary about the person looking after you. I hate feeling like this and so do others. People do not realise how important a decent nursing crew is to you and I personally feel that this is a necessity to people like myself, for comfort and rehabilitation. Being comfortable makes things cosier all round for nurses and patients and it is not fair on the nurses too, if they have to look after someone who they're not happy with, or if they know that the person that they are looking after is unhappy with them. I know that it is difficult in finding comfortable relationships between nurses and patients, but it's not impossible.

I have been through many instances where I have had nurses that I don't like, they do know this and some of them tend to play on it and either be spiteful to you, or generally wind you up. I have been threatened by several nurses in the past, but they have done this on the quiet with no witnesses, and some of them have been just plain spiteful. I have reported many of them and on some occasions the nursing staff, I have told, have not believed me, and they have had to find out from other witnesses, such as another patient or nurse, when they have been overheard. Sometimes staff have not believed me, and I have had to involve my family to sort it out for me, by confronting them or approaching the sister or nurses in charge at the time. Some of them have said " Are you sure that Carl has not misunderstood them?" but my family have said to them on every occasion, "I don't think anyone can misunderstand on so many instances." One of them that I reported denied it all, but I did have a witness, a nurse who was looking after me at the time actually overheard it and backed me up when the incident was investigated. The culprit was then transferred somewhere else.

On another occasion I had a nurse threaten me with my life and I had no witnesses. When I reported it they realised that I don't make things up and they transferred her straight away, without warning, but several other minor incidences have just been monitored. This has made me very aware of who is looking after me. From then on I have had to question every new member of staff I have had about their qualifications, their ability and their patience in looking after someone like me.

Sometimes you can find out within the first hour on duty if they are really genuine because you pick up good vibes, I have had this before and felt safe and secure. But I do know that many nurses don't like being questioned in any area about themselves, but I know I have to do it and I now make it a habit of mine. I'm afraid that if my questioning upsets people then they shouldn't be looking after me. If someone is really competent and their attitude towards patients is good, they should be happy to answer my questions. I know that it is difficult finding the right people but it is not impossible, and it can be done. They are out there. I personally think that I am a very easy and fun loving person to look after because I am not rebellious or bad tempered or rude. I am very cheerful and I am caring towards other and I have been told that I am very easy to look after. As I know everything about my care I am able to instruct people, I have had plenty of experience! I can even tell some nurses things that they don't know, and in some areas I can be more experienced than they themselves, but they won't admit it. I may not be as qualified as they are, but I certainly have the experience behind me, but some nurses still don't like, or won't accept the idea of someone unqualified questioning them, or knowing more or the same as them.

I am normally very cheerful but there are times when I do feel quite down, especially if I have had some bad news, or had an argument with a member of staff who has been either nasty towards me or uncaring. Many people who have got to know me can tell straight away if I'm not myself, as I go very quiet and loose my appetite. Some nurses who know me quite well, will often ask me if there's anything wrong with me. It may be because I don't want to cause any trouble or I just want to be left alone, but my family always pick this up normally straight away. And if I don't tell them what's wrong they either get very angry or upset, and I don't like to upset them. I don't like to see them unhappy and arguing as that also upsets me, but I know that they are looking out for me and trying to look after me, which I love very much. I do feel that I always need the support from my family, but I don't like telling them if there is anything wrong, in some situations, if they are feeling very angry with the way I'm feeling.

If something's happened then they tend to approach people to find out what's happened and what's wrong with me. When they've found out, either from nurses or patients, they want to know why I haven't told them, so I have told them that I don't like upsetting them. But they've told me "But it upsets us seeing you upset, and if you don't tell us then we can't sort it out."

I do try to tell my family about any problems, but sometimes if a problem is with a member of staff, and they are around at the time, then I cannot feel that I can tell them my problem there and then, but I'm really dying to tell them. But if they know that something is wrong, and generally they do because they know what I'm like, they start approaching people to try and find out what's going on, and sometimes I may not have even told the staff what's wrong. So what

I then do is, I either speak to my family on the quiet, or we go for a drink somewhere and I tell them then, or I just ask them to phone me later, and I tell them then.

The reason why in the past, I have not told some of the staff I've had a problem with them, is because some of them don't seem to care, or they are not really interested, so you get the impression that the majority of them are all the same, but that's not normally the case. I have had some very good caring nurses who are very understanding, and they do try to sort out my problems, either by discussing it thoroughly with me or with my family.

I must say that I have had some very funny episodes and good times with some of the nurses that I get on with, especially when it comes to making me comfortable in the chair or in bed, because on some occasions I just can't get comfortable. It gets to the stage where it gets quite comical, but some nurses get very angry but I cannot help it if I'm uncomfortable. Some of them have stormed off and left me, which upsets me terribly and I say to them "Do you think that I love being this way, it's not my fault so don't get angry with me." With some of the nurses who I do get on with, we make fun of it if I have slipped down the bed, or if I'm wonky in the chair, they will say to me "Carl what have you been doing, you look as though you've been pulled through a hedge backwards or been skiing on a giant slalom."

This does make me laugh and these are the people that I like to get on with, and get on with naturally, especially a carer called Gordon at Stoke, who was often looking after me and who used to throw things at me for a laugh. And another carer called Jesus, who I also used to joke with and swear at him a lot in his own language. He was a Spanish guy and he used to put a bet on for me or get my lottery ticket and he said to me "Carl don't forget, if you win, don't forget Jesus," and that used to make me laugh!

While I have been in Beckingham Court I have really enjoyed going to the pub called The Swan, which is just down the road. I have been there on numerous occasions for drinks and meals and have got to know many of the regulars, and I must say I think that I am going to be one. I have been down there with the nursing staff, my family, in my van and on foot. I go in the van when the weather is bad as I cannot walk down there in my chair as the rain will end up blowing my ventilator up, which I would rather do without. So now whenever I go there and go through the doors they all say "Hello, Carl," you could say it is now my local. I'll probably end up getting my own tankard because I'm always in and out of there on a regular basis!

What I really do need for myself is a mobile phone for when I'm out and about because you never know what might happen, and if I am in trouble then how can we call for help? As I have said before, to me, a mobile phone is a necessity and not a luxury. I would also like to use it within the home, as the cost of using a mobile phone has come down quite dramatically over the past few years and as I've said before, the phone in my room is too expensive for my pocket. I am so pleased that I now have my own vehicle and I've told everybody before on numerous occasions, I do feel that I am more independent now and it's so nice just to get out, whereas before, getting out was quite rare and had to be planned quite a while before going, so that it gave the nurses time to get used to me and also for them to arrange the time for them to take me out. A lot of them had to take me out in their own time, which I did appreciate, but I just wish I could have got out more. But now I am out in the community, I can basically go out on the spur of the moment with less planning.

All the way through my time in hospital I had many presents and cards for Christmas and birthdays, from members of my family, even distant relatives, and also some of the nurses, but only the ones that I got on with. Getting presents and cards used to really cheer me up especially when I started receiving them from people that had heard about me or read about me in the papers. And it is really nice that I am still receiving cards all the time and it seems to be ongoing as are the newspaper articles about me. I do enjoy all the publicity, as I told people before, it cheers me up and makes me have something to look forward to and makes me realise people out there do care. I have tried to reply to everybody that has written to me or sent me cards. I have often asked my family or other parties to do the replies if they can, but I don't know how many of them I have replied to. But I do try, but on some occasions their address has not been given, or is not clear, so I have been unable to reply. What I have done and will continue to do, is to thank people by placing a message of gratitude in the newspapers. So that people I have mentioned, or that I have been unable to write to, can see how grateful I am from the newspaper article.

I have had several reporters come to take photos of me and take messages from me. I have thanked everyone, as well as all of the reporters, for regularly following me wherever I've been, whatever I've done and whatever has happened on my behalf. When I received my TV it was photographed and published in the papers and I have had many other donations, which have been or will be published. In fact anyone who does anything for me, however small, gets mentioned in the papers. They all seem to be catching on to me and I do like to know that I will be appearing in the paper in the future. The publicity that I receive is not only for myself, but I do it to show other people how things can be done and how to go about it all, and how I try not to let things get on top of me and to give other disabled people encouragement to do things. I think this could be a stepping-stone for other people in my situation who need a lot of support and cheering up. I think my experience works wonders and this is the best way to let everyone know how you feel and make people aware that, there are many sad people out there like myself and many of which are less fortunate than myself. I do believe that having a good family and plenty of support helps you through things, and helps to get you what you need, and what is right.

There are many people out there who I think should get together and have regular meetings, to discuss their feelings about their disability and what can be done to help. I personally think that something like a Disability Club would be a good idea, where many disabled people, family and friends could get together and discuss their problems and their needs, and write off to charities and companies to see if they could help in any way, financially or emotionally. Many advocates that are allocated to people like myself can do this for you, but they don't always seem to have the right enthusiasm that you require. A lot of them can be very busy with other clients and may not necessarily get the time, but it doesn't mean that they don't care, but a lot of advocates can be overloaded with other things as well as their own lives. But if you do have a good advocate who is willing and dedicated to yourself and does have the time, then this is an excellent opportunity to use that person to help with charitable events, or to help you to get in contact with other people similar to yourselves. But I personally think the best way forward is with your family, as you can relate to them in all areas and they can give a good feedback on what's going on and how far they have got, as many advocates may keep you informed, but only when convenient.

I am glad that I do have a loving family helping me through things, and when I did receive my van, this made the newspapers write about me even more. Publicity does wonders for people and it's amazing what you can find out and what you can receive from various people. Some people can give you helpful advice and information on how to go about things, such as finding a home, or transport, or what you are entitled to, or even where there's entertainment that caters for disabled people. As you may know, I received my van through finding out that many hospitals and ambulance drivers sell their vehicles every now and then, so I think that I will try to do this with other things that I need.

I had some more publicity when I received my van. The reporters came out as they heard about this and took photos of my two carers and I beside the van. So this was in the papers to make people aware that if you shop around there are places and people that can help. This is what I have been doing with my family all along and it is gradually paying off. It is to also thank the people involved, and I personally think that this is a good idea for people in my situation, who unfortunately have had a stroke or something similar. Many people, who have had accidents, get an insurance award and can support themselves financially. But many people in my condition have no money and could use this to their advantage, and I think that something like this opens many doors and opportunities to people in my situation.

I do know that many people like myself who have no money, are entitled to benefits, but these are at a fixed rate for everyone and they do not necessarily cover the cost of everything, as some areas are more expensive than others. For example, if hiring or buying a vehicle, the money that you get from mobility doesn't always cover things like insurance, running costs or maintenance, because most of your money would go on purchasing or hiring it. So, if there is not any way of buying your own vehicle then applying to charities or enquiring about a second hand one is a very good idea.

Fund raising is another way of raising money for a vehicle, by getting family or friends to help to raise money by doing jumble sales, charity walks or even pub events, this catches on well. The information then gets passed around to other customers and other pubs who may be interested, because at the end of the day they're doing their "bit" for charity and they do get themselves advertised at the same time in the newspaper or other means. It's very good publicity for them as this kind of thing draws in customers. I do think that this idea is also beneficial to other places, such as superstores. I have heard that my family are eventually going to go to as many shops and stores as possible to ask them if they would care to donate an item from their store towards a charity raffle, then all the proceeds can go towards my appeal. Hopefully many stores will donate something so that we can have a "mega-raffle", so that all the money raised will make people see that things like this are a good idea. As well as sponsoring, at the end of the day, every superstore gets the publicity they want and I personally think this is another good way of raising money.

When you are in hospital many people who are not as well off receive very little benefits, basically hardly worth talking about, and I do know that that can be trouble. I have been there but do try to keep on top of it, so encourage family and friends to do whatever they can to help to get you get things that you need, which you may not be able to afford or are even too expensive for your family to buy. I do think that benefits should be looked into from other areas, because all they see is that you're being looked after in a hospital and they possibly think, "Why do you need money?" But you still need to live and buy clothes, toiletries and entertainment and I think that they overlook all this, but are not necessarily able to do anything about it.

I think it would be a good idea to also help people like myself, to introduce a special benefit – independent to other benefits, which can allow people like me who are not financially well off, to do things to make their quality of life happier and to allow them to buy luxuries and things that they need. Had they been well and employed they would have been able to purchase life's necessities. They may not have even prepared for something like this – because like me I did not expect something like this to happen. I thought I was extremely fit and well so I never even thought about planning or paying into something that can help you if you become disabled. I am sure there are many people who feel the same way I do about not asking, or depending on family or friends, to buy things for you. Why should you need to ask when all along you have supported yourself? A lot of people may find it easy to ask their family or friends, and they may be willing to help, but that is not the point because a lot of families may also be in a similar situation financially, and cannot help you.

I really do hate asking people for help, but really I don't have much choice and I look at it in a way that to me it is degrading, but I do try to cope as well as I can, and this is another obstacle that I could do without. The financial situation can be another contribution to things like depression, which I'm trying to avoid and keep on top of, because I have been there before and I will not go there again! I am doing quite well, I have mentioned before my many counselling sessions and I am gradually learning to cope with it myself, which isn't easy.

My condition often causes short-term memory loss and it is very frustrating for the family and the staff as well as me. When this happens I can forever repeat the same question and they reply, "You've just asked me that." The staff were concerned, and they arranged an appointment for a special memory test, but my problem is short-term and I'm very good at remembering numbers. I had a number test and the idea was that I had to remember as many numbers as I could, and had to repeat them as they said them. So they started by saying two numbers and I had to repeat them, gradually increasing the amount of numbers I had to remember and repeat to the Specialist. This went on for a while and since I was good at this test the Specialist decided that I would have to repeat the numbers back to him in the reverse order! After a while the tests had to stop because the Specialist had run out of tests! He told me that my memory is fine, but I did tell him that it was very short-term memory loss but not all the time and mainly with things one or two days before, so really the test was a waste of time.

I write things down all the time, as I may have mentioned previously as I prefer this as I then know where I am and what I've got left to do, and I tick things off when I've done then. Otherwise I will forget and get confused and then have to try to remember all bloody daylong! This drives me round the bend so a diary is a very good idea – writing a thing down is a good way of remembering. DIARIES ARE GOOD! I do also keep everything on file, for example my TV licence, bank statements, bills and other letters; this is a good way of keeping everything together without loosing them. This is also a good idea as then you know what has been sorted out and what hasn't but, it would be bad luck if you were to loose your file! I do hope this doesn't happen to me otherwise I will be doing my head in trying to think of things all day long and I'll end up saying - "I give up, I cant bloody think what I've got to sort out!" So investing in files, diaries and a note pad are important and I strongly advise it especially if you are like myself.

One thing that I've found quite amusing and has jogged my memory is one day I was out and about and I saw a group of vagrants that were writing things down, and this reminded me of a couple of people I used to know who were unhygienic and quite large, and we used to call people who were unhygienic, "FALK," and large people used to be nicknamed, "JABBA," because of the monster in the film "Star Wars" - a very large monster. The thing that made me laugh was, these vagrants were large and dirty and I told a group of friends that I was with about the Falks and Jabbas, and one of the guys I was with shouted out "Oh look there's some Falkyfied Jabbas!" I laughed that much that I walked into a man who too looked a bit trampified and I said to him "Sorry Falky!" Everyone was laughing, apart from the man who was looking rather puzzled. While I'm on the subject of dirty things I remember clearly that many years ago I was down my street by an alleyway chatting to some friends. It was quite dark and all of a sudden something jumped into the air and landed on to my shoulder and then ran off down the alleyway

- it was a rat. I nearly had a heart attack because I shouted out "What the bloody hell was that?" It was racing at a speed where it looked like it would beat a Ferrari in a race, and as the rat ran away I shouted out "You lump of Falk!" I actually got the name Falky from a guy who seemed to be strongly against washing and that's why I called the group of vagrant's, Falkyfied Jabbas!

Another thing that has jogged my memory about rats, is when me and my brothers all lived together in a house that my parents moved out of, because they had a house in the school grounds that they were caretakers of. We had a garage where we used to keep our black rubbish bags and we'd leave them outside for when the dustmen came, but they didn't turn up for a few weeks and our rubbish bags attracted wild mice. Then one day when we moved the rubbish, the mice were running everywhere so we had to put them in some shoeboxes and take them down to the brook near where we lived and let them go. Then we had to call out "Rentakill", in case there were any others roaming about anywhere. While we're on the subject, when I was in Stoke Mandeville on quite a sunny day I sat outside with my family and, because my eyesight wasn't very good I was watching a load of birds and I thought they were rats, so I starting screaming out "Look at this load of rats!" and my family said "Carl they are bloody birds not rats!" and I did have to laugh.

Quite often when I am in bed at night I have a tendency to reminisce and I often think of other hospitals I have stayed at, and how poorly I was, and also the other patients. I also think about a lot of the nurses that I have seen during my stays in hospital. When I was in Addenbrooks, even though I was poorly, I still remember incidents. I vaguely remember a man called Garth, I am not sure exactly what was wrong with him but whatever it was it had affected his personality and he kept doing and saying funny things. Even though I couldn't laugh or do anything at all I was aware of what was going on, and I was laughing inside. He would often get up out of bed and 'piss' in the sink, I couldn't see it but I could hear the voices around me and I got to learn to picture things from hearing. I heard the nurses trying to stop him from doing what he was doing, and telling him to get back into bed. One thing that made me laugh inside was something he said to one of the nurses, he said to her

"Nurse when I go home will I be able to play the piano?" and she replied, "Yes I don't see why not." He then replied, "Oh, I don't know how I am going to do that because I couldn't bloody play it before!"

I could also hear another patient, an old Chinese man. I am not sure of exactly what was wrong with him either but the only English words he could say were "Water" and "Daughter." He would say this all day long and he forever had a yanker sucker in his mouth. It kept making me laugh. Even though I couldn't show myself laughing or smiling I was doing it inside me, but I've got a feeling that after a while I think he did eventually pass away. Another comical incident that I can recall was in Papworth, when a nurse called Sarah, who was quite well built, went to pull the lamp so she could see and pulled it off the wall. And there was also my brother Darren, who can be a little bit clumsy, he actually was squeezing a stress release ball that was full of sand, but as he was squeezing it, it exploded all over me and I was very stressed, so the stress relief ball did actually the opposite and I had to be cleaned up thoroughly. My same brother also leant on the air release button on my airbed, which made the bed collapse onto the ground taking me with it. I wondered what the hell was happening as one minute I was in the air and then the next I was on the ground! The bed then had to be re-inflated which only takes a couple of minutes, but it wasn't funny at the time, but it is now and whenever I look back on it. One other incident that I found quite comical was a time when myself, and Darren were having an argument in the kitchen and I was making a sandwich. To shut him up I decided to get some butter onto a knife and flick it behind me and the butter landed on his forehead and slowly ran down his face. I was in hysterics on many occasions.

Whilst out and about in my wheelchair I have often "popped off" the ventilator, which will naturally alarm as I am disconnected, so then I am unable to breathe. When this happens I would make a "raspberry" clicking sound with my mouth to draw attention to tell people that I am off the ventilator, but many times I have been out and they haven't heard me clicking, but have heard the alarm. On many occasions when I have gone past lorries and they are reversing with their alarms sounding, the carers have thought that the alarming was me "off the vent," so they have been running around trying to find out why I am alarming, but it's not me at all because otherwise they would see flashing lights, and they would definitely hear me making my clicking sounds because I do it loud enough.

Quite regularly, if I've been out, especially if I've been in a dry sticky atmosphere or a smoky one, my exhalation filter might have to be cleaned. It has to be cleaned routinely as it can sometimes stick so it then has to be cleaned by running it under a tap or using some sterile sponges. It is easy to see whether it is clean or not, and you can also hear that it is sticking.

When I first came to Beckingham Court the humidifier that I was given was a cooler one, which varied the temperature by itself roughly about 37c to 37.5c, which I found too cool. I did have this model in Stoke Mandeville and I kept blocking off quite frequently. It happened every couple of days and I had to have a trache change so they then issued me with a hotter humidifier, which is set on 40c, which is what I prefer and what I need. When I had this in Stoke Mandeville I never blocked off again. The only time I had a trache change was just routinely, because the hotter humidifier worked wonders for me so I can't now do without it. I also blocked off even without humidification on a regular basis but the cooler humidifier didn't seem to make any difference. That changed quite quickly after my family had a lot of arguments to get the humidifier that I needed, but this is what has to be done to get you the things that you need.

The reason why I started having a humidifier is because I did keep on drying up and blocking off and also I often sleep with my mouth open, which dries up my throat and vocal cords, so that when I wake up I have no voice for a while. The hot humidifier rectifies this. During the day I am transferred from my wet circuit to my dry circuit, which means throughout the day I have to have 2 - 3mls of saline put down my trache in order to keep me moist. When I had the cool humidifier I was still putting down saline as well and I was struggling badly. I still have my Bricanyl nebuliser on the humidifier and off of it, to help open up the bronchial in my chest, and this nebuliser does also make my breathing easier and makes my chest feel less tight.

You must also be aware of any leakages within my tubing or the ventilator otherwise I won't be getting the volume that I need because the air will be escaping and not getting into me! It may be from a loose connection somewhere, or even a hole or a split in any of the tubing or even from the ventilator itself.

Since I have been in hospital I have made several visits to the dental clinics or had the dentist visit me. I have managed to keep my teeth in excellent condition due to my visits and with the aid of my electric toothbrush, which is an amazing invention as this enables the carer to get everywhere and without too much effort. It vibrates in a circular motion, quite quickly, in the same way as a normal toothbrush and I have noticed how much cleaner my teeth are now. I had never used one before my stroke but I would never go back to a manual one again. I then rinse my mouth out with a glass of water and a straw, then I have the water sucked out with a yanker sucker connected to the suction machine, and this gets rid of all the water that is in my mouth. I have tried spitting the water out into a bowl but quite often I do tend to miss, I prefer to have it sucked out.

I have made a couple of visits to an optician since my stroke, as before I never needed to, as my eyesight was quite good. Since my stroke my eyesight has deteriorated and I have actually been registered blind, but it has improved slightly, but it is still impaired. Many opticians I have seen have studied my eyes, but they cannot really see where the problem lies, as I have tried many lenses, which do not really make any difference. So the problem must be somewhere in the brain, meaning that maybe the signals are not getting through properly.

Since I been disabled I use an electric shaver, where as before my stroke I always used a wet shave. But even though the electric shaving is, I find, not as thorough as wet shaving, it's more convenient and easier for the carers and myself, as there is no messing about with foams, lotions and worrying about cutting the skin. I do often get long black hairs that are quite thick and do not seem to cut with an electric shaver, so when they are quite long I then have them plucked out with a pair of tweezers. Initially, when it is pulled out, I feel a slight sting but this does fade off after a while. I often get very long nose hairs that protrude outwards; they get long and curly at times if left for quite a while. It looks as though I have a moustache growing out of my nose, so I invested in getting myself a pair of nasal clippers. They look like a pen with several little blades on the end that vibrate and are battery operated. It doesn't hurt at all, if anything it tickles, but it does trim down the hairs within the nasal orifices.

I actually had to learn to cough again as I lost the ability to do so. I practised quite regularly as when I coughed it first started off as a slight murmur, but the more I practised the stronger the cough got. I eventually taught myself to cough up a lot of white secretions, especially if they were deep down or within the throat. I cannot cough up if the secretions are too dry. Sometimes I may need assistance with coughing. This is done by the carer shaking my chest whilst I am coughing, or pushing upwards near the diaphragm. I can often give myself an assisted cough by having a spasm and coughing together. I have found coughing useful, especially if it is to lead to suction and this also means you can have fewer suctions during the day. I still require suctions if I am unable to reach the secretions, but suctions are still needed quite regularly to maintain easy breathing and to overcome fewer chest problems. The majority of people with tracheostomies require suction on a regular basis, but this varies from person to person.

I gradually got my ability to sneeze again, this also came back slowly and started off as a very feeble type sneeze. It got stronger as time progressed. I still sneeze just like anybody else, and sometimes I also sneeze or gag if the suction catheter is tickling or irritating my trache. But when I sneeze I do not make any sound at all, whereas before my stroke when I sneezed I could wake the dead and this would leave a few tears around my eyes. I still get tears in my eyes after sneezing and also when I am yawning, but I always ended up with tears in my eyes after yawning, even before my stroke. In the early days of my stroke I often got trapped wind in my chest, stomach and bowels, whereas now I can release the wind through burping and other means. I couldn't do it when I was quite poorly. I often had to have a drainage bag at the end of my nasal gastric tube so the air could escape into the bag and could then be released. I also had quite regularly, the air drawn out of my stomach by syringe.

Sometimes this would take quite a long time and they would get up quite a lot of air, but we always knew when the air was released as it would be less painful, as trapped wind can hurt. I also often drank peppermint, which is good for trapped wind, but when you get air pockets of trapped wind in your chest it is quite difficult to get rid of. The only way of trying to get it out is when you have suction and you hope it will come out with the secretions.

Many times I have had chest problems in the past, not so much now, but when they did occur I had to have something called Scope. This is a long tube with a light on the end and a kind of magnifying glass, where you can see on the chest to see what is happening and if there are any problems. This can be uncomfortable and traumatic, especially if you have to be ventilated in one way or another. I also had problems releasing wind down below, which needed a Flatous tube to release the wind. This is a long catheter type tube, which has to be inserted professionally, with a lubricant into the bowel, and this tube has a bag on the end that traps the air within it. This can also be very traumatic and uncomfortable. With any type of catheterisation, if it is not inserted properly, it can cause bleeding.

Many spinal injury patients are unable to feel their bladders or pass urine themselves, so they have to catheterised. Catheters come in many sizes, as everyone is different. The catheter is inserted into the bladder and the urine is automatically drained out, through the catheter down the tube, into the leg bag or night bag. The catheter can go into the bladder via your urine output device. I have had a catheter once when I was really poorly and had to be transferred into another ward, but I would never like to be catheterised ever again as I found it uncomfortable and painful, due to the fact that I can feel.

There was a time when I found that my ears were getting clogged up with dry lumps of wax so I initially tried cotton buds, which removed some wax, but not all. I was prescribed a softener to soften the wax to enable it to be syringed out. This is done with warm water from a fat syringe and flushed through the ear allowing the wax to fall out into the bowl. This did not work for me and the cotton bud was tried again. More did come out and when the doctor looked into my ears with his torch he did say they looked a lot better, which I was quite pleased with, but from then on I have made sure my ears are cleaned thoroughly and regularly with a flannel and then dried properly.

In the early days after my stroke, I had to learn to talk again which was very traumatic and quiet difficult at first, but I persevered, with the help of a Speech Therapist, who teaches you how to do different mouth movements and exercises and teaches you to enable you to speak fluently and correctly. I did actually learn to do a lot of this myself and gradually got my speech back again. Mouth and speech exercises are very good to encourage the facial muscles to work properly, but one other thing that did make it difficult to talk was my facial twitches that I used to get. I was told it was usual to get after a stroke and can last for months, even years without going properly. Lucky enough my twitches went after a while. I don't remember exactly how many times I saw the Speech Therapist but, another way I learnt to speak was with a trache with a voice box which I have mentioned before, but I didn't use it much as I didn't like it as it made a sound like a Darlek from Doctor Who. These are placed by the vocal chords and detect the vibrations by your mouth movements.

In the early days I often felt quite sick so I was prescribed an anti-sickness injection. There are several types but this one was injected into the stomach and does relieve sickness quite well as I hate being sick, but I eventually went onto Dom-peredone or its' other name, Motillium. This is an anti-sickness tablet, but I now feel I can do without it as I very rarely feel sick now and I am very pleased about that!

I often used to get high blood pressure, which was regularly monitored by a B.P machine, which is a pad with a Velcro strap that goes around your bicep, which is then inflated quite slightly. It can detect what your blood pressure is - this can also be done manually, with a stethoscope, which they listen to and time the beats with a stopwatch. They can then detect your blood pressure as it is displayed on a B.P scale, which comes with it. I do prefer the electric ones, which inflate by themselves and display the B.P reading onto a digital screen. This machine is quite expensive, but I find it excellent and it can also have a satsometer built into it. I hardly ever have my B.P taken anymore as it isn't necessary, but if I did have high blood pressure again they would give me a liquid to put under my tongue to lower it. It will not work if I have full bowels, in growing toenails or something similar that would cause the pain causing the high blood pressure. It may help slightly, but really the only way of lowering your B.P, if you had a full bowel for example, is to rectify the problem - in other words to take away the pain by opening the bowels or removing whatever may be causing the pain.

Headaches are another cause of high blood pressure and the liquid under the tongue could also rectify this, as well as the painkillers. There are many painkillers about, some are mild, some strong and some need professional authorisation, such as morphine. The painkillers I have used in the past are Diplefenick or Paracetamol. This situation is called "Autonomic Dysreflexia." If you do not rectify the problem, you can have a stroke.

Quite often in the past, when trying to find a sheath that suits my needs, I often used something called a "posey" or a "uriphix strip" around the conveen to help secure it, as I did not know how good or strong some of the sheaths were. I have tried many sheaths from the basic conveen to a Warner Secure, to an Aquadry. All these sheaths do have a self-adhesive strip on the inside, but it's hard to tell which one is stronger than the other, so during an examination I would use the posey or uriphix for extra protection. This helps help hold it on as I can pass urine at quite a high speed! The posey and uriphix are like a padded ring of fabric which can help hold the sheath, they are very similar to either plasters or some of them look similar to a woggle, which is a leather type buckle which is used by scouts to put round their neck scarf.

Since I have been paralysed I have also found I have a problem with eyclashes, which have a tendency to eventually fall out. Many times one has fallen onto my cheeks and also straight into my eyes, which drives me barmy, as I will twitch all day long trying to get it out but sometimes I am unable to do so. So I then need help from somebody else to do it for me, either by trying to flush it out with some kind of eyewash, or to get it out with some tissue. It is relieving when it's eventually out. One other thing that I do remember whenever I've got pain, was my cuffed trache, which has a balloon on the end of it, which can be inflated or deflated. To deflate it would give you a voice, and to inflate it would stop you from having a voice as the balloon inside the cuffed trache inflates over your vocal cords. If it was inflated and I screamed out in any kind of pain, no one would hear me as nothing would come out. Sometimes if I tried to scream loud enough, or if there was a little leak somewhere, then the balloon would deflate to give me a voice, and as I have mentioned before this is what I initially had in the early days. It is inflated or deflated by a syringe, as it is deflated the voice then appears and when it is inflated the voice disappears. I thought that I would mention this, as when I was in some sort of pain, for example, eyelashes causing me irritation, I would eventually be able to manage to let out a noise or scream.

When I was in Papworth I was given a Bottulin injection, its nickname is called Box-Tox, this injection was to ease the muscular spasms that I get in my left shoulder, which has a tendency to pull upwards. Sometimes when the spasm pulls the shoulder upwards it can cause a little pain and discomfort. The injection was to ease the spasm and pain, but what it does is paralyses that part of the muscle and it makes it more comfortable when the paralysis wears off. But I found that it didn't do anything for me, in fact it made it slightly worse. But the only way now I find to ease the spasms and pain, are painkillers and anti spasm tablets, along with arm stretches, which the physio does. While I was in Papworth I was offered an alternative treatment which was an operation involving cutting the fibres near the muscle tissue so that it would stop the shoulder pulling upwards due to the spasm in the muscle, which has also caused my scapular, near the shoulder blade area, to twist and cause my arm not to bend at the elbow joint, when the arm is in the sitting up position.

Basically the arm and shoulder is locked into an arms length position and will not sit in an armrest in the normal fashion, so that is why my left armrest is adapted so that my arm can rest comfortably, even though it still pulls upwards due to the spasm. I then have to have my arm and shoulder pulled back down, so that my arm is comfortable again. I did not fancy the operation with having the muscle fibres cut, as I was unsure of the outcome of the operation. I may have been reassured and did have the whole procedure explained to me, but I was still worried about having it done. And also, I was not guaranteed what the actual result would be, and if it would be entirely successful, and also if I would lose any feeling, so I opted against it.

In the early days, when my eyesight was bad, I had to rely on people to tell me the time, so a patient that I got to know at Papworth, called Jerry, who was a professor in many things such as computers, made me a talking clock out of a computer mouse, which I would operate by moving my head onto the mouse button, and that would activate a voice and tell me the time. I may have mentioned this before, but this exercise did cause me a lot of pain when having to move my head, especially when I had to move it towards my shoulder, with the increased spasm in it. This would cause me excruciating pain, especially when I was unable to pull my head back to normal position, which is why I used a head roll or rolled up towels to hold my head over into a comfortable position.

One thing I have found very hard to deal with, but I am accepting, is trying to tell my body to get up and walk, and it just won't listen to me. Many times this has upset me and made me feel depressed and every now and then I do get like this, but I do keep on top of it, as there is not much I can really do about it. I have asked many people to try and imagine themselves not being able to move and every one of them has said to me "I couldn't possibly imagine it, and I don't think that I could cope as well as you do." Because I am paralysed I still need special ways of winding down and relaxing all my joints and muscles, and I do this by placing my hands and feet in a bowl of hot water and having them stroked whilst in the water. This seems to make my muscles and joints relax and feel supple. Another good way of relaxing is aromatherapy and some herbal remedies, but it's knowing the right ones, and how to do it.

Throughout my life I have had many instances where I think that I might be slightly psychic. Many people do laugh at this but I have been in that situation a number of times. You may call it 'déjà vu' or coincidence, but I always feel that I have something extra inside me. It's hard to explain, but I often feel it and the only people that I can relate to, who believe in this sort of thing, are people that experience it themselves. I have always thought that I am a bit special and a bit different, and others have told me that I am too. Every now and then

I do see visions of things happening and then either the same day, or maybe weeks later, the things that I have sensed do seem to happen, but not always in the same order that I have sensed it. And also, I am very superstitious and I do believe in bad luck and good luck.

When I was in Stoke Mandeville, part of my rehabilitation was to start going out again and mixing with other people in the community. It is a very big step and I do feel that people often stare at you, but I'm not sure if they're staring because they're curious, or just being rude. But every time that I do go out I feel this way, even now, but not as bad as in the early days. But it does take a lot of courage to make those first steps and I have been to many places, such as shopping, restaurants, into London for the day, museums and visiting friends and relatives.

Whenever I do go out and fancy a shopping spree, I always find it difficult buying presents for friends or relatives for special occasions, as my income is so low. Because I'm living in a nursing home, they look upon it as if they're the ones who are looking after you and providing your food and everything you need. But you still have to live, especially buying things like clothing and toiletries and money for going out as well as little luxuries. So it is very difficult for someone like myself, especially with the fact that I can no longer work and provide myself with an income.

Many people I think expect you to rely on your family to provide you with things, or friends, whereas I do not like this idea at all. I want to provide things for myself and not have to rely on others to do this for me. I do not feel that this is necessary, and it is also degrading and I think that people look at you in a different light and treat you as a charity case, which I do not want.

Since I have been disabled I have got paranoid from time to time and very conscious about myself. I cannot help it, but I often think that people are talking about me, or like I mentioned earlier, just staring at me, and I do hate feeling this way. But it is very difficult to overcome sometimes, in my situation. I don't always feel this way; it is generally when I'm feeling a bit low about myself. But generally I do try to keep happy and cheerful and not only for myself, but for others too. I have always been very polite and apologetic, but since I have been disabled this has come out in me a lot more, and I always feel that I should be like this all the time. But I don't always get treated any better for it, and I have seen many people who are more fortunate than myself and they have a terrible attitude, always swearing and upsetting their carers or their nurses, and I have never been this way. I look upon it as the people that look after you are trying to help you out, so being rude towards them I feel isn't going to get you anywhere and, you will only possibly end up losing all your carers or nurses. They may feel that they don't want to look after you ever again.

Wearing comfortable clothing is very important, especially if you can feel, like myself. Whenever I get dressed I have to make sure that all clothing is on me properly without creases, and there are no buttons or zips on anything as these can mark my skin, and there is not much point taking the risk. You must also make sure that all your clothing is baggy and not too tight, as this can also mark your skin. And not only that, tight clothing could cause you to spasm a lot and I always make sure that all the clothing that I buy is extremely comfortable e.g. I do not wear things like jeans, denim shirts with buttons and zips all over and I don't wear trousers. The items of clothing that I find comfortable are baggy extra large jogging trousers, extra large socks and also extra large T-shirts and sweat shirts, all these items I find comfortable. I also wear trainers, which I must buy one size bigger to make sure that my feet have plenty of room, as smaller trainers make me spasm if they are too tight. I cannot wear shoes at all, apart from trainers, as they are too uncomfortable and if I spasm I could bruise myself if I kick my legs. I also make sure that whenever I go out I wrap up in warm clothing and also wear a fleece jumper over the top and a woolly hat and a green blanket. But I would not wear these if there were a heat - wave, I probably would wear a sweatshirt and T-shirt outdoors as I do not like to expose my skin too much to the sun as I burn easily. This could cause me many problems, even more now than if I was not disabled, but even then I would still protect myself. I have to take extra precautions from now on. It is a definite pain in the arse because I would like to dress 'summery' like everyone else, but not only do I burn, but I also still feel the cold even if it is a sunny day, as somebody like myself cannot control a body temperature as well as anybody else. I also have to wear sunglasses in the summer as my eyes are very sensitive and I end up squinting all the time.

When I was in Stoke Mandeville I invested in getting two cushions covers as I was making do with one cover for a while and, if I was to have an accident in my chair, either a conveen blow out where I am covered in urine, or a bowel accident, it is difficult getting the cushion cover clean again immediately, so I make sure I have a spare one in case of accidents. The only difficult thing is, if I was to have an accident when I'm out and about, I would have to sit in whatever I've done until I got back home, as there is no way of being able to clean myself, put clean clothing on, put on a clean cushion cover and also clean the cushion itself, as this has to be sprayed with a special disinfectant to make sure the cushion is thoroughly clean.

I have developed a good relationship with a lot of the night staff in every hospital that I have been in, as the majority of them put you back to bed and deal with things like washing, tidying, putting equipment away and putting things on charge. Everywhere that I have been I have had my favourites, those who I really get on with and have a good laugh with, but I have also met several day and night staff that have been so lazy and unpredictable. And also some had bad attitudes and some of them had not got a clue about having good bedside manner. I do tend to try and avoid the ones I don't like and compensate the ones I do like and get along with. There have been a lot of nurses that I've got on really well with and truly miss, but there are others that are total shit bags and who I don't miss at all. And a lot of them act as though they've just been discharged from the army as a sergeant major! But I tend to blank those ones out and ignore them, otherwise, if I retaliated in anyway then I only wind myself up and get stressed out and that doesn't do me any good at all. So what I tend to do, and have done in the past, is ignore them and make funny jokes about them, without them knowing what I'm on about, which I find very comical and it winds them up. I think that someone in my situation, dealing with relationships in this manner is a better way than shouting and arguing and upsetting yourself, but I have had many arguments in the past with many people, nurses and patients. But sometimes it makes me feel good and other times it makes me feel even more angry, so a lot of the time I let them get on with it and totally ignore them.

Whenever I'm out and about for the day I do tend to get a lot of condensation building up in either the tubing, filter or catheter mount. I believe this is quite normal and the best thing is when you get home to clean it all or even better, change it all. And also sometimes, if I am in a smoky atmosphere, I can still taste and smell smoke in all the tubing when I get home. So I prefer to change it all to prevent any little problems that may arise, but I do tend to try and avoid busy and smoky areas.

One of the problems that I have encountered while being disabled, is how to make sure I am completely dry after being washed or showered, as this can cause my skin to crack, or get sore especially with somebody fair skinned like myself. One good thing I've found is that at least I know if I'm wet or dry because of the sensation that I have all over. A lot of people that I have come across think that you are winding them up when you tell them you are not fully dry, but that is not the case at all. I'm merely making sure that my skin is dried properly and taking care of it, which I can only do by telling the carers what to do and how to do it.

Throughout my time in hospital I have had to have my vent settings changed a few times as I have felt that the stronger I've got, the bigger breath I need, as this has gradually increased over the past four years. My tidal volume has been adjusted over the years from about 0.700 litres to 1.4litres H20 and also my respiratory rate has been increased, starting at about 8 - 10 breaths per minute and now I am on 14 breaths per minute, with a tidal volume of 1.4 litres. This is what I am happy with. It is a nice deep breath and 14 breaths per minute is roughly what everybody else breathes. I have had to change my low setting alarm from 14, down to 12, because when I was sleeping I was keeping my mouth open so the air would escape and drop below 14, which would then cause the vent to alarm. All of these settings have had to be adjusted over the years, but I have now found a comfortable setting I am happy with. And this goes for all the settings, from the tidal volume of 1.4 litres to the respiratory rate of 14 breaths per minute, and also the low alarm setting is now at 12 and the high alarm setting, which has always been set on 50. I intend to keep the settings as they are now for good. While I am on the subject of talking of settings on machines, I must also mention the saturation machine that I only seem to have on when I'm in bed at night. The saturation machine measures the amount of oxygen in my blood, and my pulse rate. The pulse and sats will read lower if the finger probe is not on the finger or toe properly. It will give a very weak reading. But the sats will naturally drop if I have a chest problem or if I need suctioning and the pulse rate will go up if I'm naturally having palpitations.

Some people may have a high pulse rate or some may have quite low oxygen sats, or a low pulse rate, but good oxygen sats are anything between 95% up to 100%, and a good pulse rate is roughly between 70 - 80 beats per minute. But one thing I should mention, which has humoured many people in the past, is that when I urinate, my pulse rate goes down, and this can drop down to anything as low as 40 beats per minute, which has worried many nurses in the past if they are unaware that my pulse rate does drop when I urinate. This can be quite comical, especially if the nurses are running around panicking, it may be the fact that the probe is not on properly, but 9 out of 10 times it's because I'm urinating. One other funny thing that does sometimes happen is when I'm concentrating on urinating, my sats go up, but on some machines that I've had in the past, after I've finished urinating the screen goes blank and the pulse and sats rate read zero, which panics the nurses even more, but the screen does return to normal within a matter of seconds.

I have been in the newspapers and on the news quite regularly since I have been making progress. I've also had many photos taken during my time in hospital. I have also had photos taken of me with the van that we brought and some taken down at the Army assault course, as they were raising money for me so I can buy things that I need, like a voice activated computer and other things. All my fund raising that's going on for my appeal is going to be an ongoing thing and many people are getting to follow all the events that I attend. They either follow it by showing up at an event or reading about me in the newspaper, and it's fascinating how there's so many people out there that are interested in me, and do actually care. Hopefully I will attend more of these types of events in the future, as they will help me socialise and meet other people. I would love to do my bit for charity for others as well. I have attended a charity line dance in Halstead, which was also to raise funds for me. One of them who took part was a friend of my mums whom she has known for years.

Quite recently I decided that I would like to go back to my first hospital that I was in when I was very poorly, this was Addenbrooks, in Cambridge. When I went back I saw their faces. I had never seen them before, I had only heard their voices as when I was there I couldn't see. It did seem that I was only there yesterday and they were so surprised at how well I looked and how well I had progressed. One thing that I clearly remember was the doorbell which you had to press to let them know that you wanted to come in, and hearing that bell again brought back many memories, and a lot of it is still very clear. I was told that Addenbrooks actually had a big shopping centre in the hospital grounds, but I never saw this. When I returned for the visit I saw the shops clearly and went round them all, and while I was there I had a bite to eat in one of the Burger King restaurants, which is not far from the hospital. My family had told me all about the shopping center, which they call the 'Concourse,' but actually being able to see it shows how far I have progressed, as in the early days I was very poorly. Even the nurses, seeing me arrive there and chatting to them, couldn't believe how far I've come. I went to Addenbrooks with my family and carers in my van, it took about two hours to get there but the drive was very straightforward. My family told me that driving that route brought back memories and they could not believe they could remember all the roads to get there, it only seemed to them like yesterday. I would definitely like to visit again, as well as to visit the other hospitals I was in.

It is very strange how my short - term memory is often affected and I do lose that quite often. I can't help it and I can't explain why it happens, and also a lot of doctors don't know why it happens. The fact that every now and then I suffer with short - term memory loss, but my long term memory is normally quite good and rarely affected. Maybe it's got something to do with my condition, or my stroke. I have had many tests in the past and everybody is still scratching their heads because they have found nothing wrong.

I am very strong willed and I am going to try and get through all of this. Yet I do get upset, and I do envy other people who can walk and breathe, but I am not going to give up. All I can do is take one day at a time and try not to dwell on the past. I would love a miracle to happen, but I know that it won't, so all I can do is hope that I have an eventful life and try and live happily and pray and hope that my life is not shortened by any more misfortunes. I really do hope that I live for as long as anyone who is quite healthy and fit, and as most people do live to a ripe old age all I can do is to wish that the same thing will happen to me. I don't want any more bad luck or misfortunes to happen to myself, or my family and friends.

Comical Events That Have Happened Throughout My Life

Insects

All insects make me nervous now that I am paralysed.

A spider fell on my belly and when the nurse tried to flick it off it went under my arm.

Once when I was able to walk, I had a wasp buzzing round me, so I punched it and it never came back!

When I was a young boy I knelt on a bee and it stung me.

Mark was whistling one day and a bee flew into his mouth.

A bee chased Darren and he threw his ice cream over it.

One day myself, Darren and Mark went to do a house clean in a house that had been abandoned. It was a contract that we had and when we went in there the whole house was swarming with fleas. As soon as we stepped into the bungalow they all jumped up off the floor and onto our clothes. We ran about scratching as we left the house, drove home and had to strip off outside and put our clothes in black sacks and be hosed down before entering our house. Also the car had to be thoroughly cleaned, but the clothes had to be thrown away as they were totally infested in fleas and that was well bad luck!

Dad, Darren and I went for a walk one day and Darren tripped over barbed wire and fell in dog mess, and then fell in a river, and cut his lip.

We were also chased by an old lady, waving a broom at us and shouting, "Get up your own end of the street." I tripped over a hedge and got poked in the eye with a branch.

One night I screamed when the neighbour's cat jumped on my bed.

A friend called Jason, who I used to know, got chased by a swan, because he was teasing it. The swan wouldn't give up until he got hold of him and the swan was screaming and having a go at him, but Jason was just running off continuously laughing.

I let Darren drive my car and he crashed it. He also drove over a landscape, which had just been done. I hit a car as I was going round the corner. I hadn't scraped the ice off the windscreen properly - my car was a wreck.

My mate Dean once drove through a barrier when taking me to work and smashed the windscreen, but as we were heading towards it, I ducked and passersby were laughing. Many years ago Dean and I used to play on the fruit machines. Dean got very angry once and punched the machine so hard he smashed the glass. Once I got angry and poured my drink over a fruit machine and it blew up. I ran away and we got barred from that pub. Dean and I also got barred from another pub. Dean had lined up ten bottles of Special Brew and downed them all in one go. I found him in the toilet, green, lying on the floor covered in vomit. The toilet brush was in his hair! We got the taxi home and Dean fell through his front door and I stayed with him until he recovered. We did laugh a few days later.

Dean has been my friend ever since we were about four years old. I do believe we will always be friends, and we still keep in contact even now. I have had many other friends, a lot of them I have lost contact with, but I am glad that I have still got Dean as a friend.

One day many years ago, when I was just a little boy, I was helping the papergirl deliver the papers. I said that I would deliver on down the bottom of the hill. I was on my bike at the time and the brakes weren't working and, I didn't realise how steep the hill was and also how fast I would go down it. I went tearing down the hill like a maniac and, as I went to apply the brakes they seemed to fail, and my handlebars were shaking all about from left to right.

Eventually my handlebars started to come off and I ended up flying over a wall at the bottom of the hill and landing in someone's garden. I walked back up the hill crying my eyes out with a fat lip. The papergirl walked me back home so that I could get my lip seen to!

One day Dean and myself were playing football down my street. Dean kicked the ball straight at a moving car and it hit the windscreen, and the ball rebounded into the air and bounced continuously on top of the roof of the car. The bloke got out of his car and gave chase and Dean and myself were running for our lives, but never got caught. A couple of days later, myself and Dean were playing darts, and we decided to have a laugh by unscrewing the top of the dart and placing it point upwards in the road. A car came along and ran over it and the tyre exploded. The driver chased us and caught us and marched us home. We had to buy a new tyre for him!

My stepdad Mark, dropped a concrete boulder on his toe and was in agony for days, which I found very amusing. His toes were black and blue and were throbbing for days. Darren slammed his hand in a door and it was black and blue for ages and he was in pain for a long time after.

These little accidents are very funny whenever I think about them but, they weren't funny at the time, especially to the person who was involved!

Dean and I were camping with the scouts once and Dean got shot by an air rifle. He fell to the ground and we all thought he was just messing about. The air gun pellet made a hole in his shirt and bruised him. We never knew who had fired the gun, but what was funny was that Dean dived like a goalkeeper - it was funny at the time but it was still bad luck.

One day I sat down on a drawing pin and it went in my backside. I jumped up instantly and pulled it out. It was quite sore but luckily enough I had had all my injections.

I cannot believe the bad luck that I have had happen to me throughout my life. Do you think that I might be due some good luck in the future? Because the law of averages says that it might happen and it should, but I don't bloody know when!!!! One bit of bad luck that I found hilarious did actually happen to somebody else, which seemed to be quite rare. One day Dean and myself were playing darts in a pub, the dart missed the board and went in some bloke's foot - he leapt in the air shouting and screaming, swearing all the names under the sun. You may find a lot of these events quite bizarre or comical, they do make me laugh and I do hope that they are funny to other people who read them.

POEMS

Throughout my time in hospital I often used to make up my own poems and then write them all down. I have always considered myself to be a bit of a poet, as you may or may not find out in a moment. Some of them may be a little bit daft but I think that a lot of them arc quite comical, and also everyone that I have told them to has also thought the same thing.

YOU MAY THINK ONCE OR YOU MAY THINK TWICE BUT I THINK THAT MY POEMS ARE NICE SO PLEASE CARRY ON READING IT ALL. I'M REALLY QUITE FUNNY, BUT NOT A FOOL, I'M CREATING THESE POEMS FOR YOU ALL TO READ, SO PLEASE DO LAUGH OR YOU'LL MAKE MY HEART BLEED.

POEM NO 1:

There was a young man from Spain,
Who used to live his life down a drain,
One night he popped out when there was no one about,
But he slipped and fell down again,
He then decided to give it another try,
But he got kicked in the head by a passerby,
He then decided that enough was enough,
And to stay down there living his life as a scruff.

POEM NO 2:

There was a young man from up North,
Who got married off to a dwarf
The night that they went away,
She thought he was a bit gay,
So she decided to have a divorce.
The night they got home, they both felt alone,
So they got back together by force,
They thought it was best to see how it goes,
But what happened next, nobody knows.

POEMS NO 3:

There was a young man from New Delhi,
Who used to eat bowls full of jelly,
He went down the pub to get some grub,
But he got stuck in the door with his belly,
He tried to breathe in, to fit through the door,
But he got kicked up the arse,
And fell flat on the floor,
He then got up to see who was there,
It was a group of lads who could do nothing but stare
He asked them politely, "Why did you do that?"
They said, "We couldn't get in, because you're too bloody fat."

POEM NO 4:

There was a young man from down South,
Who never used to talk with his mouth,
He went out with the lads, for a giggle and a laugh,
And the lads shouted out "No, he talks through his arse."
So they lined up their beers and downed them in one,
But got barred from the pub for having such fun,
They couldn't understand what they did wrong,
But neither would you, if you were half gone.
So don't ever become a true lager lout,
Otherwise you'll be left alone, with no one about.
Some may think that they're big and tough,
But those who do can't decide when enough is enough

POEM NO 5:

There was a young man from Rome,
Who used to go about with a gnome
He used to look after it, day and night,
And was forever polishing it, so it was clean and bright.
He used to take it out to the pubs and the shops,
And once in a while, he would buy it some lollipops,
Everybody thought that he was going round the bend,
But all that he wanted was his own little friend.
He used to get upset when everyone laughed,
Especially when they would shout – "He's bloody daft!"
At the end of the day, it was his friend for life,
So much so, that he loved it more than his wife.

POEM NO 6:

There was a young man from France,
Who used to go about in a trance,
Whenever he went, people would stare,
And the crowds would shout out "Hey you, over there!"
But no one would realise that he was in his on little world,
So jokes and comments at him, would be hurled.
At the end of the day, he kept himself to himself,
And was lucky enough to enjoy good health.

POEM NO 7:

There was a young man from Greece,
All that he wanted was a bit of peace.
So he went for a walk, all alone,
He didn't take any money, or even a mobile phone.
Eventually he got lost and had nowhere to go,
Where he was nobody knows.
So take this warning, or a bit of advice,
Don't wander off wherever you like!
If all that you want is to be alone,
Then please tell others that you'd like to be on your own.
Otherwise they will not know where you are at,
So be a good boy and don't do that.

You may think that people don't care,
But how do you know, if you're not there.

POEM NO 8:

There was a young man from Brazil,
And wherever he went he was ill.
Everybody used to look and stare,
And most of the time pretend he wasn't there.
He couldn't understand what he'd done wrong,
For people not to stop and help him along.
He always used to offer a hand,
And deep down inside he was a kind man.
All that he wanted was a few good friends,
Every now and then, with a hand to lend.
Deep down inside he was a good bloke,
So don't wind him up or even provoke.
At the end of the day he could be a friend for life,
So treat him with respect and talk to him nice.

POEM NO 9:

There was a young lady from Wales,
Who was forever cleaning her nails.
She'd scrub them in the morning, evening and night,
And she was always tempted to give them a bite.
She adored her nails, even though people stared,
And she used to think they never really cared.
People would look at her beautiful face,
But she always thought that they looked in disgrace.
At the end of the day she loved to look nice,
And all the men she would entice.
It would be nice to be with her all through my life,
But she cannot be mine, as she's already my wife.

POEM NO 10:

There was a young lady from the States,
Who used to sell top quality plates.
She had her own shop and her own market stall,

She specialised in top names and catered for all.
She designed them herself, all on her own,
And even placed orders from over the phone.
She shipped them places, near and afar,
And would do this herself in her company car.
At the end of the day she was a good housewife,
And she has been forever doing this throughout her life.
I don't think that she will ever give up,
Because she's decided to make a new line in cups.

POEM NO 11:

There was a young man from the Isle of White,
Who slept during the day, and woke at night.
He tried to be normal so that everybody cared,
But people used to laugh and others stared.
But at the end of the day it wasn't his fault,
As deep down inside he was a really nice bloke.
To himself he was normal, and others weird,
As he was the only bloke there, with a seven foot beard.
So that's one of the reasons why people would stare,
But at the end of the day, he really did not care.
He was a lonely man, who lived by himself.
And he couldn't give a monkeys about anyone else.
He was a decent man who people would neglect,
And all that he wanted was a bit of respect.

POEM NO 12:

There was a young man on a vent,
Who couldn't afford to pay his rent.
The landlord said – "I'll give you a warning,"
And the young man said; "I'll pay in the morning."
He rang up his dad to borrow some dough,
But his dad said, "Son, I really don't know!"
It wasn't his fault the way he was,
As misfortunes do happen and I'll tell you because.
Whatever he did, he did from the heart,
And he didn't expect to be torn apart.

He is a really nice man, but he can't take the cold,
But he always thinks of others, as he has heart of gold.

JOKES THAT I HAVE COME ACROSS

JOKE NO 1:

There was an Englishman, Irishman and a Scotsman, all stranded on a desert island with nowhere to go. They found a bottle on the beach, so they opened it up and out popped a Genie. The Genie said to them all "Thank you for releasing me, I'll give you all one wish each." So the Englishman said, "I would like to go back home and go down the pub with all my mates, and have a jolly good time." So the Genie said "Your wish is granted." and he disappeared. The Scotsman said, "I wouldn't mind being back at home with all my mates, eating and drinking to our hearts content." The Genie said "Your wish is granted." and the Scotsman disappeared. And the Irishman said, "I want my mates back!"

JOKE NO 2:

There was a man on a desert island. All he had with him was a dog and a pig. He took a fancy to the pig, and wanted to make love to it, as he was a lonesome man being on a desert island for several years. But whenever he tried to get near the pig, the dog would go for him. But one day a beautiful woman got washed up onto the island. She was unconscious so he gave her mouth-to-mouth to revive her. She eventually awoke and looked at the man and said, "Oh thank you, is there anything, anything at all that I can do for you?" He said, "Yes, take the dog for a walk.!!"

JOKE NO 3:

There were two nuns decorating their house and they got covered in paint. They'd got no other clothes apart from those they were wearing so they said to each other, "We'll have to take all our clothes off so we can wash them." Suddenly, there was a knock at the door. They could not open it as they were naked, so they decided to shout out, "Who's there?" A man replied, "It's the blind man". The two nuns said to each other, "Oh, that's ok, we can open the door, he won't be able to see us." The man looked at them and said, "Nice tits ladies, where do you want your blind put?"

JOKE NO 4:

There was an Englishman, an Irishman and a Scotsman, and they are all very curious about their neighbour as he never leaves the house, but he is always making money. So one day they look over at his house, and see him standing in his garden looking up at the sky. So the Englishman says, "I'm going over to ask him how he makes all his money." The Englishman goes up to him and says to his neighbour, "We are all very curious about how you make your money when you never leave the house." So he said, "Well, my friend, I shall tell you. Early every morning at about 6 o'clock, I let all the bees go and they fly over the park to collect nectar and they bring it back to me so I can make honey and that's how I make all my money." So the Englishman replied, "Oh, I see," and he went home to tell the other two. The Scotsman said, "I think I'll double check, I'll go and ask him." The Scotsman comes back and says to the Englishman, "Yeah, he told me the same thing," and the Irishman replied, "You two are gullible, he's winding you up," and they both say to the Irishman, "What makes you say that?" And he replied, "I will tell you why, because that park does not open until 9o'clock!"

JOKE NO 5:

There's a man who bought himself a miner bird, but whenever he tries to talk to the bird, it just swears at him. So he says to the bird, "Don't swear at me, or I'll put you in the freezer." So he then tries to talk to the bird again and the bird swears at him again. So he says to the bird, "Right, I did warn you, you're in the freezer." So he puts him in the freezer, and the miner bird is running around in the freezer, trying to keep warm. He looks down by his feet and he sees a frozen chicken all packed up and sealed. And he says to the chicken, "Bloody hell, what did you say wrong?"

JOKE NO 6:

A man goes into a pet shop and he says to the owner, "How much are your wasps?" And the owner replied, "What are you talking about mate? I don't sell wasps." The man said "Oh yes you do, you've got one in the window."

DREAMS

Since I have been disabled there are many dreams I can remember, but quite a lot of them I can't. However, the ones that I do vaguely remember, I have been in, but not walking, and not in a wheelchair, but I have just sensed I have been there. It's as if I was a fly on the wall, or a spirit. But I am actually within the dream somehow. Whenever I wake up I always forget them, but I can still remember some dreams that I have had before I became disabled. I can honestly remember some dreams I had as a baby, and they have been with me on many occasions throughout my life. I find that very strange especially when you are growing up and a lot of your childhood memories fade away. But with a lot of things that happened to me as a youngster I have not forgotten and some things I have, but I do often if I am quiet, drift off into my own little world and reminisce about things that happened to me in the past, or as a youngster. I think that dreams that are intense and quite real you never seem to forget. One dream which I do remember since I have been in hospital is a very clear, but quite frightening experience. Whenever I talk about it it does make myself and others laugh.

The dream that I encountered on this occasion was a dream where I was being chased by a lot of men waving club hammers and baseball bats. I remember myself running down an alley whilst being chased. In addition, I remember waking up in a panic, sweating, and saying to myself, "Thank gawd for that it was only a dream." However, five minutes later I have fallen back to sleep and I have appeared back in the same alley and they are all waiting

96

for me! They have all said, "Look there he is, let's get him." I am then back on the run again being chased. Has anybody ever heard anything so strange as this ever before because I haven't. Whenever I tell it, it has people in hysterics because they cannot believe the amount of bad luck I tend to receive.

Quite recently I have had a lot of things going on in my life, which I do enjoy as I love being busy doing things, and I reckon that a few dreams I have remembered because of this. I may be wrong, but that's what I think it may be down to. Some of the ones that I do remember are quite comical, and you may think so too. Here are some of them:

I was going around Colchester but I was not in my wheelchair, I was actually walking along, carrying my ventilator under my arm.

I was going shopping, and as I was queuing up at the checkout, I rested my ventilator next to the till and I remember people looking at the ventilator as I placed it down.

I dreamt that I was on the set of the children's programme "Rainbow," and beside me was Zippy and Bungle, but there was no George the Hippo but myself in replacement, with the vent, sitting on the Rainbow table.

MY VAN

Now that I have my own vehicle I can attend more outings and events, which I enjoy as I cannot stand just sitting around all day. I like to make my new life eventful, even though it may not be the greatest thing in the world - being paralysed - but I do try to do what I can, when I can. I do have "off days", but then so do many people. When I do I don't like to involve others. I like to get through that day and put it behind me, but people can often tell when there's something wrong with me, as I become very quiet and deep in thought. A lot of people often ask me if there is anything wrong of if they have upset me in any way. I would normally tell them, or others, if they have done anything wrong, or if I have a problem. Usually, it will be the fact that I'm just in a quiet mood and in thought. I will either talk about it or I will just say that I'm having a quiet day and there's nothing wrong. I'm just thinking about the past or the future. It doesn't take me long before I'm back to my normal cheerful self. I do have tearful days like anybody else, but normally they don't last long but I have seen many people in my situation getting very depressed indeed. This also affects others around them and their families. Some people don't want to come to terms with what has happened, and others try to, but they're not always encouraged to do so. It is very difficult but you have to try, not only for yourself but for others too. I have heard of quite a lot of people in my situation feeling suicidal. I must admit there were occasions when I too felt like that. But this also has an effect on your family and friends. I am going to make sure that I do as much as I can to make my life eventful. It isn't brilliant but I haven't a choice, so I'm going to make the best of it. At the end of the day I am still "CARL" and if I make others happy, then that makes me happy too.

LOOKING AFTER YOUR SKIN

Skincare is very important especially when you are paralysed and you need others to assist you in making sure that your skin condition doesn't deteriorate in any way or form. For example, making sure that if your skin tolerance isn't brilliant, turning frequently can prevent any skin deterioration such as bedsores etc. Most people can gradually build up their skin tolerance and where most people turn every three hours, this can be eventually prolonged so that you are able to stay in one position for longer. Everybody is different, and some people can tolerate staying in one position longer than others. If a sore arises then these can be very difficult to get rid of, but this all depends on how bad their skin has been damaged. For example, if the red area does not blanche then this means that the skin is damaged and you must keep off it until the red area has faded. Blanching means that when you press the red area the blood fades and then comes back, this means the skin is alright and undamaged, but if the blood does not fade and still stays red even when you press on it, this means the skin is damaged, and then you will have to keep pressure off it until the redness has gone.

Depending on how damaged the skin is will depend on how long you will have to stay off of a particular area. It could be for about three hours and then you will have to turn. This can gradually build up over time so that you could possibly stay on a particular area longer before turning. When you require pressure relief whilst in your chair, the carers should ease you forward so that your bottom and back are relieved. This normally goes on for a few minutes, just to relieve the area. This too can be gradually built up whilst in the chair but everybody is different. Some people can take a long time to build up their skin tolerance, while others manage it quicker. Another way of looking after your skin is to make sure that your clothing is quite loose and free of any buttons or zips that may cause your skin to mark. Having loose clothing does also mean that your skin can actually breathe and this will also help to prevent you from sweating and also causing unnecessary red areas. Personally I only wear tracksuit bottoms that are nice and loose, and extra large t-shirts or sweatshirts, with socks and trainers. I prefer trainers, as they are gentler on the skin.

Other things that you have to keep an eye on is to make sure that your leg straps are not secured too tight as these could mark your legs and also cause spasms, which I have experienced myself. I also make sure my socks are quite large and that they are not too tight on my toes, so that this is comfortable within the trainer. I do get spasms all over which are natural to my condition, but I also get violent spasms when I pass urine, but some days the spasms are stronger than other days and my legs tend to jump in the air. I do take medication to keep down the spasms but they don't really have a great deal of effect. I am currently on Dantrolene capsules, but I have also been on Baclofen, but that had a tendency to make me drowsy. The same went for the Aclofen injection that went into the spinal cord - this is Baclofen in a fluid form. I do like my spasms to a certain degree as this can help to relieve pressure on areas of my body. I can also make myself spasm by shifting myself a little, which does relieve pressure areas. I do have a tendency to have violent spasms when I urinate, this can be an aggravating task especially if you have to then be repositioned. I also do like to keep an eye on my toenails as they can also cause spasms if they start to grow inwards. In fact, any pain that is inflicted on your body, in any area will make you spasm, but this can also tell you that something is wrong somewhere, so in a way spasms can tell you if you have pain somewhere or you are uncomfortable in any way.

I have never actually had any problems with my skin because I can feel and shift about a little bit. I have had marks on my hands, and these have been caused by my splints, and I have had many problems with getting the right splint, which is comfortable for me. My splints have got soft padded areas, but only on the areas that mark me. It often takes me a long time to get my splints comfortable and just right, but I only wear these overnight, but in the early days I did only wear them for an hour or two until I could tolerate to wear them overnight. I have got a soft glove, which I wear on my right hand when I am in my chair, as the palm of that hand has a tendency to get red and sore due to the fact that it has a lot of spasms in it, and has a tendency to claw up and get tight. When I am wearing my splints overnight I also have to make sure that the straps are not too tight as this has a tendency to mark my skin.

My pulse oximeter, which I have on overnight, but not normally during the daytime, has got to be positioned on my finger in the correct way as my finger tips can be hypersensitive, which makes them sore if the probe is positioned incorrectly. I prefer the probe to be on my finger but not right to the very bottom, as there is a plastic point inside the probe that I can feel. I also don't like my finger probe to be touching any other fingers as this too irritates me. Getting the probe right is a lot easier than having to keep continually moving it all the time throughout the night. Finger probes can mark, as they are quite tight to wear, but I seem to get on with it alright. There are other probes available, such as padded strips that do go around your finger, or ear probes that clip onto the ear lobe, which I have tried and found very uncomfortable, especially when you move your head around and the probe eventually slips off your ear and has a tendency to pinch it. This would also give a false saturation reading because the probe would then not be positioned properly. In the past, when I did have an ear probe, it did keep coming off and setting off the pulse oximeter alarm, which did make everybody, including the nurses, look and wonder why it would be alarming. What I would really love would be to lose the ventilator and the pulse oximeter altogether!

COMMON AND UNIQUE OCCURENCES

There are many symptoms common to ventilated people and people who are tetraplegic, such as many of them can go dysreflexic, which is a racing blood pressure, which happens when the body tries to tell you when there is pain somewhere. Many people can go bradicardic and tachicardic. This is when the pulse rate will either be very low or very high. This may occur on freak occasions or this will occur if you are hot or cold, or have drastic pain, or even if the tracheostomy is irritating in any way (if you have one) especially if somebody is applying pressure on it which will stimulate the nerves. Many tetraplegics cannot feel pain, but some of them may feel a slight discomfort. But if you are able to indicate that you are uncomfortable in any way this makes life easier on yourself and the carers, especially as they have to establish the problem. So knowing where your pain is, is beneficial to everybody involved in your care.

Many tetraplegics cannot feel their bowels or their bladder, but I do have some control to a certain degree, which is very useful all round, and can also prevent many complications. Another bonus is that I can tell if I am hot or cold, so in a way I call myself unique to others similar to myself and I do believe that many things which are written or fact do differ to myself, which again makes me in a way, a unique case. Many people have tried to relate themselves to what they have read in books, and many of them have said to me (if something is not in common to tetraplegics,) "You're not supposed to be able to do that," which either makes me giggle or makes me very confused. One other symptom that I have, which is virtually unheard of with somebody in my condition, is that my eyesight isn't normal sighted or short sighted, it's just very snowy. Very similar to if you were to pull out the ariel from your television and the picture goes snowy. This is what I see all of the time.

I can also smell, which is also very rare, as well as having sensation and some sense of pain. I am also grateful that I can also feel my bladder and bowels, as I would hate it if I were to lose this as I do have control, though not fully, but to a certain degree, and enough to relieve myself. If I needed I could instruct somebody to help me to go by tapping my bladder or evacuating my bowels. So even if I cannot go or empty my bowels fully, I am able to instruct the carers to assist me. I have also gradually taught myself to cough again, which is very useful if there are secretions within the throat, which are out of reach for suctioning. I can also sneeze and relieve myself of trapped wind, in all areas. My sensation is very normal from the top of my head to about my chest, and anywhere below that the sensation is there, but very muffled. I can feel, but not as clearly as I can from my chest upwards. Even though I am very independent, I do miss doing things for myself, especially if I have got a limb which needs moving, which I can do slightly, but not all of the time. So being stationary can make my limbs ache. From time to time they do need moving or stretching, which I would love to be able to do myself entirely. I also hate it when I have an itch and I cannot scratch it, and then have to rely on somebody else to relieve it for me.

Many people do take their health and their ability to do things for granted. This is very natural, but also it can make you envious towards others, and I have known many people to be extremely jealous of others who have all their physical capabilities and health. I must admit there have been times when I have been jealous of other people, but this rarely happens to myself now, as you gradually grow to accept your physical condition and your capabilities. There is one thing that I would really love to happen, and that is to be able to loose the ventilator. Being disabled is very upsetting and I do get upset from time to time about this. Generally I am all right and I do stay quite cheerful and optimistic. Being ventilated is upsetting, not only to myself but also to others, especially my family. I would dearly love to breathe by myself, but yet again, I do try to keep on top of this.

There is one thing, which I do find difficult, but not every time, this is when I do go out and I am amongst others. I do get very self-conscious and paranoid about my condition, especially when others do tend to stare. I don't suppose they mean any harm, but it's probably just a natural reaction. Sometimes if I am feeling low about myself this makes me feel alien to others, especially when people do stare. I try not to let it get to my family or myself, so I try to fight it and put on a brave face. Going out regularly would reduce myself feeling like this, which I do hope to be able to do in the future, but I am getting out when I can. What also helps me is the publicity I have been getting since my accident. I have regularly appeared in the newspapers and have got to know many people, some famous and some that are genuinely caring and interested in myself.

I have known many people in my situation make many new friends as well as have relationships. I have indeed met many friends, some I have kept in contact with, and others I haven't. Some have either just moved on or passed away. But I have known a lot of disabled people to encounter romance, just like anybody else. I have seen many having relationships with able-bodied partners like themselves. I have also known many to have relationships with their nurses or their carers. I personally didn't think that I would ever get involved again in a relationship and have feelings for somebody and I do remember saying to myself that I would never want to get involved in a relationship again because of my condition, as I thought that I may not be wanted. I did also feel that I might be a burden. These feelings have now changed and I have realised that being disabled does not mean that you cannot have a relationship just like anyone else. With the way I feel now I have gradually been able to build up a lot more confidence in myself and have been able to express my feelings, whereas before I didn't feel I had the confidence to do so. I have fallen for somebody who I dearly love, which I never thought would happen and I now feel very special and wanted. I do intend to carry on the way I'm feeling which is natural anyway, but I do not feel that I ever want to end this and the relationship has made my life more enjoyable, and this also encourages me to live a normal life just like anybody else. Many people in my condition have relationships but at the same time, involve their partner in their care as well, which I do not feel I would want to do, because I would be involving a partner to also look after me, which could lead to complications and arguments, especially if your partner was to overlook the other carers you had, and became critical of their standard of care. I personally think that I would like to lead a relationship aside from my care.

I do not want to know what the future holds for me, so I just try to live every day as it comes. One thing that really frustrates me is not being able to earn an income and having to rely on family and loved ones to provide things for me, which I personally feel I would like to have some control over. I know that my family and many others love doing things for me, which I appreciate, and love them dearly for it. I wish I could have some control of my income, which I personally feel I should be entitled to, even if I am being looked after in a residential home and have things provided for me by the home, and my loved ones. I would like the choice, especially when I need to buy clothing, toiletries and other little luxuries. I know that family and friends don't mind helping me out, but they shouldn't have to. I am still an independent person and an income is just as important to someone like myself, but not many people seem to see that. I think that special benefits should be awarded to people in my condition or similar, and we should not have to be treated as a charity or sympathy case.

When I have encountered people staring at me when I'm out and about, it does make me feel alien but not everybody's like this. There are many people who treat me as normal. But there are also others who go overboard and treat you and talk to you as though you are deaf or stupid, which I do not like at all. All I want is for people to treat me just like a normal human being, in all areas, because at the end of the day, I am still me, even though I am in a wheelchair. I should be able to have the choice of an income, just like anybody else, and have a relationship, just like anybody else. I do treat others as equals and I do not look at others and think that they are superior to me just because they can walk, and they have their health. I may not have my physical capabilities anymore, but I have still got my mind and I know what I want, and I AM STILL CARL.

VOICE ACTIVATED COMPUTER

Since my stroke in December 1996, my family and many others have been doing fund raising events for the Carl Holmes Appeal. It took a lot of organizing to get it underway, but it has all been happening gradually and many charitable events have been occurring, which I have attended. The newspapers have been interested in me from the beginning and so have many others, especially those who have heard about me.

It is amazing how so many people are interested in knowing all about me and especially with helping me for things that I need. Many people have been interested in fund raising for me and also interested generally in myself. Many of the fund raising events have been towards my computer appeal. I have also had donations from high street stores, Slim Fast and David Jason, who was kind enough to send some autographed items to be auctioned at one of the events I attended. These items were all to do with "Only Fools And Horses," like books and videos. There were also some jockey trousers, which were autographed by all of the top jockeys. My appeal is still going on and will be on-going. I have seen a voice activated computer but all it could do was print text, even then it made many mistakes. I am actually after a computer that would do absolutely everything by voice command, but the company that I dealt with told me that computers are not quite that advanced yet, so I shall be either hanging on until something more suitable comes along for my needs or try another company who may know more. I am also after a system that would operate lights and curtains etc. by voice. I was offered something that turns the television on and off by voice, that's all it could basically do. This was a square screen on a stand with a microphone sticking out of it, which resembled the robot from the "Short Circuit" film. However, this machine did look an eyesore, especially when all it could do was turn the television on and off. Also it is pointless, especially when I have a carer with me 24 hours a day.

Throughout my time in hospital I was allocated an advocate to help me through any problems I might have encountered. They are solely there for you and will help you with whatever they can. For example, my first advocate was a disabled man himself. His name was Phil Miller. He helped me with trying to find an interim placement so that it would help me to get back into the community. Many options were given to me but they were too far away from home, which meant that my visitors would become fewer and my family and friends are very important to me. Those places were basically out of the question for me. I was also offered a bungalow within the Colchester area, which had all the plans set out so that it was suitable for me and then, for some reason, it was sold off to a family, which really did upset me as I was so looking forward to getting this bungalow. After a while, Phil Miller left the position as my advocate and it was then, after several introductions (from other advocates) that I met Helen Lee who has been marvelous towards me. She has stuck by me dearly, in fighting to try to get me what I want in all areas, and she is still acting for me, even now.

I have also had many social workers who have promised me things and then suddenly left, and this does get very confusing, especially when you are trying to sort out things financially and you don't seem to be getting anywhere. The whole ordeal has been very frustrating for me especially when you don't really know where you stand and where they are coming from. Being messed about is very upsetting, not only for me but for my family as well, as they too have been very confused all along. Things get gradually sorted out, then more problems arise, and then it all seems to be a very slow process in getting what you need in all areas. At the end of the day, it is all very stressful, which is only more added worries for me. I have also been told from many parties, what benefits I am entitled to, and

I have been told many different amounts all along, which has also confused me. They are still not sorted out fully and I am basically living on what my family provide for me, which I shouldn't really have to rely on, even though they don't mind doing it. I am still an independent person and would rather pay my own way in this world like others do. But it is so unfair that I cannot have that choice, and I personally think that benefits should be sufficient enough for somebody like myself to live on.

MEMORIES - LONG TERM AND SHORT-TERM

Since my stroke, my short-term memory has been bad on many occasions. I have a tendency to get funny little vague episodes, which can last days, or can last hours, but nobody really knows why I get them. I have been told that when I have these vague episodes I have a tendency to stare into space as though I have just drifted off somewhere. People who have witnessed this have told me that I stare as though I am in a trance and at the same time I have been told that I also slap my lips together as though I am chewing something. I can never remember these episodes. What is very strange is I always have slight memory loss afterwards. There was one occasion when I had a bad vague episode and I couldn't remember why I couldn't move or where I was, and I didn't even know who my family were, which was very upsetting all round, but I did eventually recover from that. What is strange is that I can actually remember waking up after being transferred to a high dependency ward after a bad vague episode, and shouting out "Where am I?" and "Why can't I move?" I also remember a voice calling out to me and telling me to be quiet and go back to sleep, which had me in tears, as this person had virtually a non-existent bedside manner. I needed comforting and reassuring, which I didn't get. He then also told me that I had had an accident in a very abrupt manner. Then I don't remember any more after that. I don't even remember recovering from that episode.

What is very clear to me is basically everything that I used to do from my schooldays up until my stroke. I remember things like what I used to do job wise, and where I used to go with my friends and girlfriends, and what cars I've had, and where I used to go shopping. All of my personal details such as bank accounts etc. I even remember faces of regular people who I used to bump into, like in pubs and in shops. I also have many memories of when I used to go out clubbing and to the casino with all of my friends. I even remember people's names who used to work in these places, as well as many people who I got to know. I rarely hear from my friends now, but many of them have also moved on and one of my friends has moved to Australia, which I only recently found out, which did upset me a little. I have only recently remembered that I had booked a holiday with my friends to go to Spain, which we had all paid for and we had bought everything we needed for it. I did feel that in a way I had let them all down as I don't even think that they did go in the end. But I was really looking forward to it and it is really strange how you can start to remember things as soon as they have been reminded to you.

I did have some good times with my friends, especially as we were quite often out and about, and on many occasions we had good laughs when we used to go up to Blackpool or Margate on the spur of the moment. We would just hang about there for a couple of days at a time, just as though we had not a care in the world. Whenever we used to set off anywhere we would just forget about home life and enjoy what we were doing at the time, until we eventually got back. My friends and I were always doing whatever we could. Going to places like casinos and the nightclubs were so enjoyable because we always contributed to the surroundings, because we were so outgoing and enjoyed whatever we could. We would always be on the dance floors in the night clubs and we got to know a lot of the regulars who went in there, so on many occasions many people all knew each other. But a lot of people used to call me "Sogy," because of my first car having these letters on the registration plate, so that was my nickname. But if we went to the casinos or to the West End, it seemed as though you were just one of the others blending into the surroundings as we were in our hometown of Colchester. I have had so many good laughs with my friends even though I hardly see them anymore, but I still remember the good times we had and the things we used to do, and I shall never forget them.

ANDREW'S WEDDING

Since I have been disabled I have been to my brother Darren's wedding, my mum's wedding and most recently my cousin Andrew's wedding.

Going to this particular wedding was a very nervous ordeal, especially when I had to meet members of the family who I haven't seen for a long time. The build up to it had crept up on me gradually and I was so nervous and anxious with not knowing how several members of the family would react to seeing me this way after so long. I have seen a number of them since I have been disabled but other members whom I wasn't very close to, I haven't seen since I was a young boy. Some of them spoke to me as if I was just speaking to them yesterday and some of them would just stare, and I suppose that they really didn't know what to say to me, but I too felt the same way. I suppose I was really a little bit scared about what they would all think. Many of them I did get to speak to, but there were some I didn't, and others that were not really related to me. It took me virtually all day to feel comfortable being in the company of everybody, especially when I had to try to make conversation with those that I hadn't seen for a long time and also with those I didn't really know. The most nervous part of that day was meeting my uncle Norman again but, not only was it nervous for me, but for him too. We gradually started to make conversation with each other but we didn't talk about the past at all, it was all about what I do now and what I'm planning to do. I think that I may start to gradually see him a bit more now we have re-introduced ourselves after so long, I even met his partner who I also know well. It seemed very strange seeing them both together, it seemed like I was only with them yesterday.

After gradually meeting everybody I was getting more comfortable with the surroundings, but at the same time I was also getting very tired and I could no longer find the energy to stay for the evening party. I decided that enough was enough and I left with my carers and Diane (more about her later!) at about 7'o clock. When I eventually got back to Beckingham Court I was so exhausted and tired that when I eventually got into bed I was asleep virtually instantly, with no trouble at all, and slept soundly all that night. After taking it all in and meeting Norman again I had a good cry, which I really did need, to let it all out of my system. I do intend to do a lot more with my life and to also get to see Norman a lot more.

Meeting Andrew again did also bring back a lot of memories, as I did used to go out with him a lot on a regular basis and I must admit that meeting old faces again for the first time was very difficult, especially having to try to keep on top of it all. But I was going to do it, and I had to do it, and I am so pleased that I did it in the end and faced everybody. It was a big step for me and I think this made it comfortable all round for everybody.

ALL ABOUT THE POWER CHAIR

The "Power Chair" that is shown in the book is the one that I use now, and that I am most comfortable with. This is the Gillingham Tilt power chair. It is exactly the same as the one I tried out in Stoke Mandeville, which I got on with really well by controlling it with a chin control joy stick. The power chassis has three speeds, slow, fast and very fast. I started off on speed one, which is the slowest, and I'm now on speed two which is a bit faster. This speed is very comfortable to use, especially when going over rough ground. The manual chassis, which I had before, I have still got, but it is kept in storage just in case the power chassis happens to fail in anyway. The power chassis can also be switched to manual so that the carers can push the chair by themselves, but it is a lot heavier because of the motor within the chassis. The ventilator is positioned a bit differently from how it was on the manual base. It has been placed in a tray above the same battery, which is also situated on the power chair. So having the ventilator and the external battery, which it runs off, makes the chair a lot heavier than before, especially when having to push the chair up a hill or into my vehicle.

When entering my vehicle I normally have to tilt my chair forwards as the weight on the back of my chair has a tendency to lift up the front of the chair, which then makes all the equipment scrape along the ramp. So to avoid this we simply tilt the chair forward and the carers push from behind and pull from the front. This means the carer can control the power to enable me to get into the van, without the chair tipping over backwards. I can only use the

116

power chair by myself within the home and grounds. If I choose to use it out in a public place I have to have special lessons, which are given by the company, but I would rather the carers take control of pushing me when I am out, because I don't want to take the risk of hitting somebody as I have a tendency to spasm a lot, which could cause me to hit the chin control, which would be no fault of my own and unavoidable. In addition, my eyesight isn't 100% for me to be driving my chair in public.

The speed that I have it on is not too fast, in fact it's just right, as the weight of the chair slows it down a lot. The weight of the chair makes the tyres quite flat, even though they are fully inflated, which also slows the chair down. So overall the speed for myself is just right.

COMMUNICATING WITH THE FAMILY WHILE IN HOSPITAL

Being able to communicate with your family and loved ones is very important especially to someone like myself and in my situation. In the early days of my time in hospital it wasn't really practical for myself to be able to use a telephone as quite a lot of it was in high dependency units. This meant that using a phone wasn't always convenient, especially when you are poorly and there is not someone available to do it for you. Most of my visits in the early days were sprung upon me by chance, which was very nice, but it is also nice, at the same time, to have some indication of when visitors are coming. I wasn't able to use the telephone as I was too poorly and my voice wasn't really that strong, but gradually it came back. When I was in Stoke Mandeville I started to use a telephone again, as this was not possible in other hospitals. The telephone that I would use was a payphone on wheels, so that it could be wheeled to wherever you were, and as well as a handset receiver it also had a pair of headphones which you could talk into and also be able to hear. This gave the nurses a chance to do what they were doing without getting an arm ache! Also, I felt that I had a bit of privacy. But quite often this payphone was either in use, or out of order, but they did have another one, but that was often used down the other end of the ward. So if the phone was unable to be used then I often had to use the nurse's phone, on their desk, but only if I was receiving a call. But even then, I felt as though I had no privacy.

I often felt that I was being rushed as they were holding it whilst picking up their arm off the floor!

When I moved to Beckingham Court I had a similar phone like the nurses had by my bedside, although I still felt as though I had to be rushed. And also the calls in the room were very expensive, they were on hotel rates at roughly fifty - five pence a minute, which was crippling me. So I decided to buy myself a mobile phone with a headset so I could talk away to my hearts content without any hassle. Many people think that mobile phones have an effect on equipment, such as ventilators, but I have made some enquires and this comment is actually fictitious.

One of the reasons I brought myself a mobile phone is because they have come down in price dramatically over the past couple years, and they are now cheap to run as I buy cards, and I just pay as I go along, and there is no rental or any kind of charges. You just buy the phone and top up the cards every month. It is very useful having the earpiece so I can talk and listen, without anyone having to hold the phone for me. Also you do tend to get more privacy this way. I also brought the phone to take out with me whenever I'm out and about, because you know that if an emergency ever arises, you could be stuck in a traffic jam without the use of a phone. So as well as a cheaper way of communicating, it is also a lifesaver for me.

Recently there have been many arguments about whether or not my mobile phone can be used, because of the possibility of it interfering with my ventilator. But the ventilator manual stated many other possibilities of interference such as from televisions, hairdryers, radios etc. I have also had the OK to use it from other people who are constantly involved with ventilators. Recently I have been told that I am not allowed to use my mobile phone within the Nursing Home due to the risk of it affecting future ventilated patients. At first I accepted the possible risks and carried on using it, but I did intend to reconsider if they were to get any more ventilated patients. They have now made an overall rule within the Care Home that mobile phones are not to be used on the premises. I am allowed to use it when I'm out and about and when I get my own home. The alternative way of communicating would be either in person or by mail, which in an emergency is not much use if you need to talk immediately. In addition, if I had to wait until somebody did arrive, I cannot always remember what I wanted to say. At other times what I wanted to say was either personal or private and I didn't fancy somebody writing it all down for me, for when they next visited.

CARL'S HOMEMADE JOKES

Why did the spider buy a computer?
So he could get on the web!
Why did the gorilla beat up the lion?
Because he owed him a monkey!
Why did the horse beat up the giraffe?
Because he owed him a pony!
Why did the hedgehog cross the road?
To see his flat mate!
What do snails watch on T.V?
Shelley!
What is a fishes favourite pop group?
The Carpenters!
What do rabbits like playing?
Hopscotch!
What do toads like playing?
Leapfrog!
What do toads sit on at home?
Toadstools!
What do centipedes wear to keep their heads warm?
Earwigs!
Why didn't the razor blade take part in robbing a bank?
Because he wanted a cut!
What did the ants say when they saw a drawing pin?
We're under attack!
Why did the T.V dislike the radio?

Because it was a stereotype!
What did the carpet say to the curtains when they had the hump?
Pull yourself together!
What did the grape do when it got stood on?
Nothing - it just let out a little whine!

What did the dog say when he got set alight?
Woof!
What do horses like watching on T.V?
Neighbours!
What do sheep like to sing?
Baa Barbara Ann!
Where do sheep save their money?
In the Woolwich!
Why did the camel beat up the cow?
Because he had the hump!
How do lions like their meat?
Roar!

PREPARATION FOR GOING OUT

Since I have been in a wheelchair, being able to go out can take a lot of preparation, for example: - knowing that the people that you are going out with are able to carry out all aspects of your care, from the medical side, down to suctioning and being positioned properly in the wheelchair which is very important. If you are uncomfortable in any way with the people you are with, or the care carried out, it can reflect overall in the way you are feeling and it can also affect you mentally and health wise. So being comfortable wherever you go and whoever you are with, makes life a lot easier.

In the early days, if I was with somebody who I didn't like, or felt uncomfortable with, I would go very quiet, not talk or eat or drink, so it affected me overall. But I do not get that problem anymore now as I am very independent and I can instruct anybody with what I require in respect of my care.

Before my stroke, whenever I wanted to go out I just got up and went. Whereas now I have to make sure that the people I need to take with me are all available and that my equipment such as: - my chair, ventilator and portable suction machine are all in working order and that I am well. So there is a lot more to consider and to prepare. I have been out on numerous occasions, and I have thoroughly enjoyed shopping. I have also been to rock concerts, and seen stand up comedians, such as Jethro, museums, and have even been to the cinema. I have also been on a few hospital appointments mainly just for check ups. There is one place that I really did enjoy and that was the Millennium Dome. I could not believe what was inside there, it covered all ages and different parts of the world with different zones such as: - the Futuristic Zone and the Medieval Zone, which showed what it was like if you were to live in those times. They also had a few rides and many other things to look at, but what I did like was the publicity that I received. Everyone bent over backwards to make sure that I got priority in all areas. Some of the queues were massive, they stretched so far that if I had had to queue I would have been there for days. I did manage to see most of the Dome as I got priority overall, and it did make me feel quite special. I could tell that some people didn't like this, but I would rather be in their position than the one I am in now. Some people do tend to forget that they have one of the most important things, which is their health and that they are able to go out and to do whatever they like, within reason.

One of my medical visits was to St Thomas and Guys Hospital in London. I was there for a few tests and examinations regarding my kidney stones. I was meant to be there for a couple of days, but in the end I only needed to be there overnight. I was in a big unit called "Fox Lane," which had many ventilated clients being looked after by lots of nurses. I also had Di with me, (coming to that bit!) which helped me tremendously as I was with someone who could carry out my care and also had the added bonus of being with somebody who I wanted to be with, and who I loved and cared for. One thing that I do remember about my stay there was that there was another person in that unit who was in the same unit at Stoke Mandeville as I was. He recognised me straight away and so did his family. He did seem to look quite well and cheerful. He was so pleased to see me and so were his family. They asked if I was staying there for a while, I replied, "No, I am only in for tests and a sleep study," (where they monitor your oxygen saturations overnight.) I am not sure when I have to go back there for more tests and have my kidney stones looked at. The night that I did stay there, me and Di went for a wander round the whole hospital and they had a few shops and restaurants there that we went in. One of the restaurants we stayed in for quite a while, eating and drinking overlooking the nightlife of Westminster, it was all lit up. We could see the Houses of Parliament, it looked very beautiful, especially over the river Thames. It was just like a romantic dinner for two, it was so nice just to be able to be alone and I do think I am going to enjoy going out when I am eventually in my own home.

I am now in the process of leaving Beckingham Court as a bungalow is in the pipeline. At the moment it is going through all necessary channels for purchasing it, which the Health Authority and other parties are doing. I cannot believe how long it can take in purchasing the bungalow and finalising all the details. A bungalow was going to be sorted out for me a long time ago, before I left Stoke Mandeville, but for some reason it fell through, but now it is eventually getting sorted. How long it will take I do not know. But there are so many people involved in this and I do not think they talk to each other, as no one seems to know what is going on, or where they are at, which is nothing unusual. Once it has all been finalised the alterations and adaptations have to be done, so that I can enter the bungalow through wider doors and with a ramp in situ, as well as a ceiling hoist and a generator and basically all that I need and that I use now. A shower room with a shower trolley will also have to be prepared. Before I do eventually move into my own home, all my care staff who are going to look after me, will have to be trained in all areas of my care, just as when I left hospital and came to Beckingham Court. I will have to get used to new people, but once they get to know my care and me, I am sure that everybody will be happy. I do make sure that the people who look after me are doing it properly, and if there are any problems I will just correct them along the way, so being verbally independent and knowing all of your care is very handy to new staff and present. I do instruct everything that I need even if they do know it all, but it helps myself, and them not to forget.

One thing that I will never forget is when I used to live independently and did my own things, such as shopping, washing, dressing, and general everyday things. I do remember that I did enjoy all of it so I do think that when I am in my own home I will feel the same way as I did before. I do also remember what it was like doing similar things with the girlfriends that I had, and now that I have got Di I am definitely going to enjoy doing things even more than before, as we are so comfortable together and get on so well. Also one other important thing is that I am more mature now, whereas having girlfriends before, when I used to go out, was like a competition between other girls and your friends, where everybody would brag about what they did and with who, just taking things as they come for granted. Now I look at a person that I am with differently and I also appreciate their views on life as well. How you both see where you are going and what you hope the future holds. Whereas when you are younger, going out is just 'going out,' it becomes like an everyday task. The same with girlfriends, a girlfriend was just a girlfriend, but like I said, when you get older you look at things differently and appreciate what you have got and who you are with and your outlook on life is different. I suppose this does happen to everyone eventually, but I personally feel that it means more to me, which many people may not be able to understand unless they are in the same or similar situation.

RETURNING TO SOCIETY

Since I have left Stoke Mandeville I have tried to build up some kind of social rehab, which would help me to blend back into society. In other words, getting confident in being out and around other people, as some may find you interesting and others may be frightened as they may not quite understand what they see. For example, the ventilator may be the first thing that people think, "What has he got there?" Especially seeing the tubes coming out of you leading into the ventilator, but overall I personally think that a lot of people are getting used to seeing disabled people in wheelchairs, as these days it isn't uncommon. I would still like to feel comfortable within myself being around strange faces. I have been out on several occasions, but I would really prefer to do this on a regular basis, but it's not as simple as that, as it is not always easy to get staff available or confident people who can care for you.

Quite recently and also over the past couple of years, I have had many meetings with the Social and Health Authority and with my family, to decide where I will go from Beckingham Court and what kind of care package I will have. I will also have a say if I am not comfortable with anybody who is caring for me, and I will also have at least two carers on each shift so I can do the things I want and that need doing. I have now got to the stage where the Authorities have decided to jointly fund a bungalow for me, which will eventually be modified for my use with wider doorways, ceiling track hoist, a shower room and most importantly, a back up generator, in case of power cuts. Basically it will eventually be transformed for me to live in with my carers, this will be in the Colchester area. I am looking forward to it, as this is what I have wanted all along.

I will be living independently in my own home, but also with the back up of a nursing home close by, called Treetops. They will be there to help or assist me whenever I need it, so that is a comfort to me and a big weight off my mind, as at least I will know there is somebody there in case of emergencies. I am now getting what I have wanted all along, but it has been a long fight and has meant many meetings and arguments with certain people involved. They have shown me and also offered me other nursing homes that they have wanted me to go into, this was going on before I came to Beckingham Court and before Beckingham Court had even heard of me. All the ones I had visited were not really what I was looking for and also they were so far from home that visitors would be too far away to come and see me, but being within the Colchester area is so easy for family and friends and they are close at hand if I need anything.

What I cannot understand is the fight you have to put up to get what you want. I would have thought that parties involved would be only too pleased to help get you what you want. I have witnessed this over the past few years, what with all the meetings and the letters which I have had and, I have had so many people that have been involved that come and go, and it gets very confusing not knowing who is involved and who is not involved, but I'm glad that it is now virtually getting sorted out, with what I want and what I need.

My family is very pleased with the outcome and the results that are happening. It is all in the pipeline. The bungalow is empty and ready to be adapted for my needs. Before I am ready to leave Beckingham Court I will have to have a whole new team of carers to look after me, so they will have to do all of their training by either coming to work "hands on" with myself, or have some prior training with an agency that provides care packages, which is what happened when I first came to Beckingham Court. There was somebody employed from them to train up the people who were going to look after me, and I suppose the same thing may happen again with the help from Beckingham Court. One of the strange things that I've always found difficult is having to get to know different carers, but hopefully I will get a team, a more regular team who will also know me well too. I really cannot wait for all of this to happen and it is quite an exciting feeling. I suppose that I will have to have annual reviews and check ups at the hospitals, which I think is a good thing as they too can keep an eye on what's going on.

MOVING INTO MY BUNGALOW

I moved into my bungalow on Monday November 19th 2001. It had all been modified for myself to live in, with wider doorways and an adapted shower room and a shower trolley. The shower room is where the bedroom en-suite was, so I can basically go on my shower trolley directly from my bed, via the sliding sheet. I have also got a ceiling hoist above my bed to enable myself to get into my chair and also into bed. The whole bungalow has got a wooden floor, so it is very easy for the carers to wheel me about. It has also got a generator, quite a large lounge with a conservatory, a kitchen and accommodation for the carers, which includes their own bathroom and toilet. The bungalow is very well heated just incase I was to get too cold. I have always got two carers with me at all times, but it is nice to know that Treetops Nursing Home is only around the corner with help at hand if needed or in an emergency. The carers have all been given training in looking after me, in all aspects of my care, from washing, to toiletry matters and ventilation care.

I have been gradually getting bits of furniture as I go along, to make the bungalow look more homely and to my liking. It is so nice to eventually be out of hospital and to have my own independence and my own choice. It is also so nice to be in charge for once. I decided to gradually settle in and get to know my carers, and for them to also get to know me, before I start going out with them, as it does take a lot of confidence and trust on both sides.

Being in my own bungalow allows me much more freedom to do as I please. It is so nice just to be able to phone family and friends, and to ask them if they would like to come round, especially as they are all so close by. It is even so nice to be able to invite Di round and Di being able to stay overnight, basically whenever she is able to. It makes us both feel like we are a normal couple, and we are left to our own devices, but the carers are still within calling distance whilst they are in their own quarters. I do also have an alarm bell, which they can be called upon if an emergency should arise. Having my own telephone with a headset, enables me to speak to anyone in private, without anyone having to hold the telephone for me. I still have to watch my phone bill and this does apply to everything else, as I'm currently trying to get all the benefits I am entitled to. Only then can I work out what I have to pay for and what spare cash I have for going out with.

I would like to eventually be able to go away somewhere for a few days, for a short break, but I do believe that to make this possible, there will have to be a lot of thought and planning, as I will have to take several carers/nurses with me. I will also have to take a lot of supplies and equipment with me, so it will require a lot of thought. I have been told that this is possible as there are many suitable places that could accommodate me, but this will take time to arrange.

I have been given a new advocate who is sorting some things out for me and who does play a part in sorting out financial matters, as well as help from others. Everything is coming together slowly, but at least it is getting there and I can see the results. At the moment I am getting groceries and some bills paid for until everything gets sorted out.

Just before I left Beckingham Court I went to an "Only Fools and Horses" convention, where they have everything to do with the show, from videos to souvenirs. The convention was held in Ongar, which is just outside Chelmsford. I was so looking forward to going there and when I got there the whole convention was so crowded that no one could move, and there was also a four hour queue to meet some of the stars from "Only Fools and Horses." These were Denzel, Trigger and Sid from the cafe. When I found out how long the queue was I felt really disappointed, but I was so desperate to see them that my family had a word with the people in charge and I was able to meet the stars on my own in another room. I was so, so happy and pleased. I told them that I knew David Jason and that we write to each other and send birthday cards as well, and they seemed very shocked and surprised, but also interested. They did tell me that I was lucky because he never writes to them!

I decided to settle into my bungalow and to get used to, and know, all of my carers before venturing out with them. Instead of using the vehicle that my family and I brought second-hand, I thought that it would be a good idea to start using transport from Treetops, as most of my carers are insured to use their transport. I first ventured for a walk with my carers to a nearby Tesco. I was so pleased that I had made my first move back into the Colchester area since my stroke. I was very nervous to begin with as I didn't really know how people would react towards me in my hometown.

After I had made that first step I felt so good about going out, that I am hardly ever in now! I seem to get a buzz while I'm out and I feel that I blend into society well. I have been out many times since I moved in. The local newspaper has done more articles about me, some of which are included in this book. Not long after I had moved in I was re-assessed for some new hand splints, which were long overdue. Within four months of being in my bungalow I had about three pairs made for me at the same time! On each occasion, they had been lost.

I have recently been shown a brand new vehicle, which will accommodate my chair and I. There are two seats in the back for the carers or family, and seats in the front. This is in the process of being modified for me.

COMPUTER FOR CARL APPEAL

Since I have been in my bungalow I have finally decided to buy a computer with the five thousand pounds raised for me through the Essex County Standard newspaper and their readers. I got a home computer with a scanner, printer, digital camcorder and C.D re-writer. I also managed to use some of the remaining money to buy a wide-screen T.V, Video and DVD player. This I thought was a good buy and is ideal for my eyesight. Now I've got my computer I can use it to my advantage, especially when writing this book.

Before we went ahead and purchased some computer equipment, I had previously dealt with a few companies that specialised in voice activation. I had tried several of these packages, which unfortunately were very unsuccessful for me, mainly due to the noise from the ventilator interfering with the system. It couldn't pick up my voice properly, so many things that I said came out a bit strange. I would persevere with the package for many hours, trying to train the computer to my voice so that it would understand me. For example, I would practice going through the alphabet seeing if the computer would then relay it back to me. On many occasions I would say a sentence, such as " My name is Carl Holmes," and the computer would then repeat back what it thought I had said – the computer would come out with phases like "My nose is Carol Hind," the reason being, it couldn't understand me. I made several attempts to make the computer understand me but to no avail. After many failed sessions we decided this might not be the right route for me. This particular package was very expensive, and if I were to go ahead and purchase it, I would have to have several lessons to train my voice onto the computer, which would cost more money. Even if I were to go ahead with the package that couldn't quite understand me, it would also cost money to set the system up. I thought that this would be a complete waste of time and money. Others agreed with me so we decided to get a full normal computer system for the carers to use on my behalf. It consists of a monitor, a keyboard, a printer, a scanner, mouse, software, computer tower, speakers, digital camera, paper and ink. While the fundraising was going on, I was appearing in the newspapers on many occasions, so that I did feel like I was a bit of a celebrity, as I was often on the front page. There was one incident I remember, where I was out and about and a crowd of people said, "That's that bloke from the paper!" and they all turned round and looked. I did feel like quite special, and at the same time, quite nervous.

DAILY ROUTINE OF EXERCISES

I have a routine of various exercises, which I do like to do religiously. They may change or differ if I have a busy schedule, or if I am due to go out quite early. My exercises consist of several leg movements. For example, knee raises to the chest for many repetitions, but I do this with the help of a carer and this will be one leg at a time. The exercises help to minimise spasms, which can be very uncomfortable and aggravating. This exercise does also help the flexibility of my joints and prevents them from seizing up. The exercises also help to strengthen my bones. I do my exercises every morning and similar exercises to my arms and hands in the evening.

I have two abdominal exercise belts, a Slim Jim Pro 12 and a Rio Ab belt, both of which are from Argos. These help to tone my stomach muscles and burn off a few calories. I use one of them in the morning and the other at night, both whilst I am on my bed. I do not use a set one in the morning or at night, I tend to alternate them depending on how I feel. Both belts do basically the same job, but the exercises differ slightly. The feeling that the belts give is very similar to the feeling of doing sit ups. The belts do have different speeds, strengths and programmes, all of which are adjustable.

The Slim Jim Pro 12 has a range of programmes and a timer, so I can decide how long I want to wear it. The Rio Ab belt has three programmes, all of which last for 60 minutes. Both belts can be used on other parts of the body, I only tend to use them for my stomach because my legs and arms have regular exercises/physio performed by my carers. The Rio Ab pack needs to be used with a special conductive gel. This makes it more effective and prevents friction burns. My other belt has a series of self-adhesive pads, which do not require the use of gel. These pads do need to be replaced after a while as they lose their adhesiveness.

CORRESPONDANCE WITH DAVID JASON

After meeting David Jason in Stoke Mandeville I have regularly kept in contact with him, via cards and letters. I have told him about Di and me, and about getting my van. He told me that he is currently doing a few new series of Only Fools And Horses. At one of the charity events for my computer appeal, he actually autographed some Only Fools And Horses memorabilia, they were auctioned at the event. The proceeds were added to my appeal. I also hear from his partner Gill, who does some administration for him. I have grown to know her. We also exchange birthday and Christmas cards.

I am so pleased that David takes the time to not only read my letters, but reply as well, it means a lot to me. David and Gill have told me a lot about their daughter Sophie. It is nice that they want to share some of their life with me. I keep writing to David and I hope that some day, I will see him again. In August 1999 David paid me a surprise visit, which had been arranged by the nursing staff. I couldn't quite work out who it was standing in the doorway, as I couldn't believe it was really him! I said "Who is it?" and he replied "What do you mean who is it?!" As soon as I heard his voice I knew it was David Jason. I cried out "Del boy!" He brought me a few autographed Only Fools And Horses gifts.

In October 1999 David came to visit me again. He brought me a birthday card. On both occasions he called me a "Dipstick," and I called him a "Plonker!"

CORRESPONDENCE WITH THE BENEVOLENT FUND FOR HELP TOWARDS A SPARE WHEELCHAIR

Since I have not been working for the Civil Service I have needed on a few occasions, help with financial matters, such as difficult bills etc, which has been very helpful whilst I have been in hospital. I have now approached the Civil Service Benevolent Fund again for help towards a spare wheelchair, which they are considering helping me with. They sent out one of their representatives to see me in my bungalow, he went through the reasons why I needed help. I then had to wait for a decision as to whether or not they could help me. They told me that my application could well be considered. When I finished working for the Civil Service in 1994 due to medical reasons, they helped me with my debts. When they found out that I had had a stroke and was wheelchair bound they approached me and told me that they would love to help me towards something that would be beneficial to me. A spare wheelchair is always handy and is definitely a must. I have tried several wheelchairs in the past, and the one that I have now is the only one that I am comfortable with. So if anything should happen to it, I would be bed bound, until it is repaired.

Recently, a few accidents have happened to my chair. One of my armrests cracked and had to be taped to hold it in place. I also had an accident where one of my tyres suddenly exploded, which meant that I had to stay in bed until it was repaired.

I had a couple of visits from the Wheelchair Clinic, and they came with the wrong wheel for my chair, and I had another surprise visit when they came and looked at my cracked armrest.

When they measured them and told me that they should be able to renew them, I nearly fell out of bed with shock, as I had previously been waiting for months to hear from them!

WAITING FOR MY NEW VAN

When one in my situation moves into the community they automatically qualify for a motability allowance, which may be used to purchase a van. If you decide to purchase a van then you automatically go on a waiting list. This can take quite a long time, especially if modifications need to be done to the van. Some people may choose not to use their motability allowance to purchase a van therefore they have to make alternative arrangements to get one. Insurance, road tax and maintenance may be paid for using the motability allowance.

Getting a modified van can take several months, as the application is considered by, a "Motability Panel." They will notify you by phone or in a letter, if and when it is approved. You then have to wait for the modifications to be done. Before this is all decided, they give you a demonstration to show you around the vehicle and what modifications are to be done. During all of this, arrangements for the insurance should be taking place. For example, who is going to be named to drive it and what purpose it is for. The vehicle is always maintained by motability, if the vehicle has to go away at all for any repairs you will be given a replacement until it is returned.

I decided that I liked the vehicle after going in it, and after seeing what modifications are going to be made. My application form went before the motability panel and I was informed that I would have the van at the end of March 2002. I am currently still waiting for my van, it is the beginning of June 2002. It can be very frustrating waiting, especially when you're so keen to get out and cannot do so. I do hope that I receive my van shortly, especially as it is summer.

GETTING OUT

Since I have been in my bungalow I have been on many outings, shopping, cinema, greyhound racing and eating out, using the Treetops van. I do also go for many 'walks,' but on some occasions I cannot do this, depending on the weather. If there are high winds that force air down my trachea at a different rate to what I am used to, I hyperventilate. This means that I have trouble catching my breath, which makes it hard for me to breathe. Rain can also be a problem, especially with the electrical equipment on my chair. I cover these using a poncho, which also covers me; I usually try to avoid such weather.

I intend to do a lot more when I eventually get my van. I am planning to go to France for the day, to London shopping and horse racing, which I love – especially placing a bet. I have been told that if I ever decide to go away somewhere on holiday, this could be arranged as John Grooms have many places all over the country, which could cater for me. I do intend to look into this. If I do decide to go away then it would be nice to know if friends and relatives could come with me, which would make the holiday more special.

Ever since I have been in my wheelchair I have needed transport to get to most destinations. It was very easy to do when I was in hospital, as they did have vehicles that could be booked for patient use. When I left and went into residential care that facility was no longer available. So I then had to go ahead and purchase a second hand vehicle, which was an old ambulance, which catered for my needs quite well. All my family chipped in to purchase it, but I still had to wait until the family was available to take me out. There are similar vehicles that are owned by taxi firms, which you can use, but of course taxi fares work out very expensive. I am currently awaiting my new vehicle. They took me into the van and measured the dimensions of my chair, and also looked at how many clamps I would need to fasten the chair down so that it wouldn't move when the vehicle was in motion. They also decided where the carer's seats should be, so that they could get to me easily should an emergency situation arise. I am currently waiting to hear more about this vehicle, so I am using the vehicle from Treetops Nursing Home. This can be inconvenient, as it has to be booked quite far in advance, and it is not always available. This can be very frustrating.

USING THE TELEPHONE

Using the telephone can be quite difficult when you are disabled, especially if you cannot move your arms or even hold the telephone. So, luckily enough there are devices to suit your needs.

There are many on the market. Some are hands free, which means you can speak via a small microphone, or you can get a small headset that is very similar to headphones. They consist of a microphone, attached to an earpiece, so that you can speak freely. I have used the headset system before as they did have a similar system at Stoke Mandeville, which was attached to the payphone. This could be brought to your bedside, as it was on wheels. I now have a similar headset on my home phone, which is ideal, and works very well for me.

There have been some phones that I have used, where the carer has had to hold the phone to my ear, in the normal fashion. However, you feel as if the phone call is hurried along and it is less private, as the carer is there, all of the time. Sometimes it can look as if the carer is getting tired and uncomfortable. I can get on really well with the headset and I can make my own personal calls to friends, family and businesses. And, it is quite nice that the carers can then retreat to their own quarters while I am on the telephone. This makes it more normal and private.

One thing I do enjoy is, I am now making more of my own phone calls. For example, when ordering my Slim Fast, I can then take the opportunity to talk to them in general, and ask how everyone is. When I am speaking on the telephone I get a good buzz out of it, as whoever is on the receiving end quite easily understands me, even with the noise of the ventilator. When speaking to someone unfamiliar to me, I do let him or her know that I am on a ventilator, and that I have to wait to get a breath so that I can speak. I have found out that many times, the person on the receiving end will keep asking between breaths, if I am still there. On some occasions it makes me feel good when they can understand me properly, and that they do not know that I am on a ventilator, which is quite a unique feeling and somewhat of an achievement.

WORRIES REGARDING BILLS

I have always been worried about paying bills, not in the sense of trying to avoid them, but actually trying to find the money to pay for them. I have always been like that, but now it worries me even more. I am continuously worrying about bills that I have to pay for, even though I have been told that it will be sorted out eventually. It still bothers me though, as I like to know where I stand with them. I know that I will not lose what I have got, but I am still a born worrier!

There have been meetings regarding my financial situation but not all of my benefits have been sorted out yet. I am in the dark about these matters, even though I have been told not to worry. I still have the usual bills that come through the post, just like anyone else, and I have been able to pay the ones that I know I still definitely have to pay for. These include the telephone bill, TV license and some of the electrical equipment I have bought myself. These bills are included in the budget as they are classed as luxuries. Another reason why I like to know what I have to pay out for is eventually I will be losing my mobility allowance and I shall be getting my new van soon. This will then leave me with quite a small income to cover whatever I have to pay for. Outgoings will increase when I get my new van, as I will have to pay for petrol as well. I was told that my income might not be as high as others, due to the fact that some of the bills are covered in the budget. Which ones I am still not sure of yet.

There was also some news recently that I had been waiting months for. It was about the completion and delivery of my van. I have had several phone calls regarding my van, telling me when it should be completed. I have heard that things are moving along now, but it is already taking much longer than expected, as several dates have not been met. This is due to complications with paperwork and lack of communication.

I have also had a few phone calls regarding the insurance. I need to have an, "open policy," so that any of my carers can take me out in it. I will need to know the age restriction for the drivers, which hopefully will not be too complicated.

WORRIES ABOUT EQUIPMENT FAILURE

One of my main important worries is equipment failure, which has happened to me on several occasions, particularly with my ventilator. One incident occurred in hospital where my ventilator packed in altogether, and just decided to stop working. Naturally I started to panic and tried to call for assistance by making the raspberry noise that I make when I am in trouble. The nurses came to my aid immediately and started to bag me so that I was still breathing. That particular ventilator was sent way to be repaired and I was given another one. However, the replacement was one of the old LPIO's, it looked like a small chest. The worry about my ventilator failing is continuously on my mind, but I do know that there are people around me that can keep me breathing with an ambu-bag, until help arrives. I have had many ventilators taken away and looked at for faults, and also for general servicing. They then replace the vent with a temporary loaned ventilator. One of my ventilators was recently sent away for servicing, and I was given a replacement for it, however, the replacement was very sensitive to high pressure. My current ventilator had been altered so it was not so sensitive. The loaned ventilator was alarming every time I coughed or had a spasm, which drove me barmy and kept me awake all night.

So what I have had to do if one of my ventilators goes in for repair is to use just the other ventilator, which then has to be taken from chair to bed everyday, day and night. This is very strenuous and stressful for the carers and myself, as I have to be bagged while the ventilator is being changed from the dry to the wet circuit, or vice versa. This has also caused added worries because, if there was a fault or failure with it, I would be left with the over sensitive loaned one. When I get my ventilator back, the spare one that I use is serviced as they can only service one ventilator at a time. There has been an occasion when both my ventilators have not been fully functioning, which then results in calling out the engineer, and me being bagged until the engineer arrives. Most of the engineers are "on call," so they can be reached at any time, day or night, however, they are not always able to sort out the problem straight away, which I have experienced before. In this case I am given a temporary loaned ventilator.

I also worry about the ventilator tubes being pulled or coming loose. This will then create a leak, resulting in me not getting a full or deep enough breath. The tubing to the humidifier seems to pop off quite easily now and again. I have also had humidifiers that have not been operating fully. These will alarm and not heat the water. On one occasion I was given a replacement, but that particular one was very basic, and would only heat the water to 37 degrees. I am used to 40 degrees, so my secretions were actually setting like jelly, as the temperature was not high enough. This resulted in my trachea blocking off, so I was unable to breathe.

This would happen a couple of times a week. I would then have to have a complete tracheostomy change each time this happened. I now have two humidifiers that I am used to, so that if one does fail, I always have a back up. However, I do still worry that I may eventually get the cooler one back again.

One other thing that does have to be kept an eye on, is the bag of sterile water that feeds into the humidifier. I have had in the past, bags that have run dry and people not realising that the humidifier has burnt out. I have also had people change the bag, not with sterile water, but with saline instead. This means that the salt in the saline crystallises in the humidifier, making it unable to function to its full potential. On other occasions the bags have not been pushed down in the giving set properly, which has resulted in the water trickling down the outside of the tubing and straight onto the floor. This can be highly dangerous if the water falls onto the humidifier itself, or onto the electrical wires coming from it.

On many occasions my sats machine, which measures the oxygen levels in my blood and my pulse rate, has suddenly alarmed a high pitched sound, which is different to the alarm which sounds if your sats or your pulse rate drops. This particular alarm occurs when a lead or a wire becomes disconnected from the machine. Some people are not aware of this, as the alarm is unfamiliar to them. At one point, I did not know what the alarm meant either, but I am now able to tell others.

MONITORING FLUID INTAKE

Ever since my stroke, and even before, I have always been one to drink plenty of fluids to flush out my system and to keep infections at bay. Since I have been in hospital, they have never kept a check or recorded, my daily fluid intake, or even monitored the output. I believe that this was possibly not noted due to the fact that I was drinking large quantities. This changed slightly when I went to Beckingham Court, as they decided to record my urine output, but they never did record the fluid intake. The same thing applied when I moved into my bungalow. They kept an eye on the output, and also the colour of the urine, and if it had an odour. They would test the urine by using Diastiks and Albustiks. These show if the urine is infected, or if it contains traces of blood. These tests were done daily, and the test for the blood was done weekly.

Recently, I have been having my fluid intake recorded, which I think is a very good idea, as you get a rough idea if you are retaining fluid in any way. This also makes sure that the kidneys are functioning well, especially if the fluid intake roughly matches the urine output. If my urine seems to have a slight odour to it, then this usually means that I need to drink a bit more to flush my bladder and kidneys through.

One thing that has not been decided yet is, whether they're going to regularly monitor my kidney stones, or whether they will operate on them, or laser or blast them. I have been told that they will decide the best way for them to go, but I am a little concerned by the fact that it has been roughly about a year since I have heard anything regarding them. If they wish to just carry on monitoring the performance of my kidneys and the size of my stones, then I am more than happy to do that, but I would like to know what is going to happen.

The thing that I am very concerned about is that, if I were to leave the stones as they are, and just have them monitored regularly, would it make surgery more difficult, or more traumatic at a later date, if it is required? Or, if I did decide to have the operation, then, could this also make the situation worse by disturbing something that has been there for a long period of time, and which has not given me many problems lately.

MY GARDEN

After about roughly six months of living in my bungalow, my front and back garden started to look like a miniature jungle. So members of my family did a total transformation and clear out, which they did over a few days. I could not believe the rubbish that was cleared out. The rows of black bin liners that were stacked up full of weeds and other garden waste, which took several trips to the local tip to dispose of. When they had completed the garden, it looked quite presentable. Keeping it presentable all year round would be a difficult task, especially in the bad weather. The best time when it can be worked on, is during the spring and summer, when I can go out and observe, as cold weather is not good for me, especially if I have to be outside for a long period of time. It would also not be appropriate for my garden to be worked on with me being left inside and out of earshot of my carers, in case an emergency should occur. The funny thing is that if next summer the garden is left, it will get in the same state again. So this is a difficult situation to overcome.

I was told that a group of students from the local college might be interested in doing a makeover of my garden and including it in their studies, but I never heard any more from them.

During the summer I went and purchased a bar-be-que and a gazebo, which was erected in my back garden. I have been looking into buying a garden heater for the cooler evenings and I do think that a patio heater would be a good idea. I have actually used the bar-b-que, which I thoroughly enjoyed, as I have not been able to do this for many years.

VEGETARIANISM

After being in my bungalow for several months I gradually decided to give up meat, and turned to more vegetarian and Quorn based meals. With added flavourings and herbs I have found that I prefer Quorn, as it has a nicer texture and flavour. I still do occasionally have chicken if I go out for a meal, and I do still enjoy some fish, like scampi and prawns. Some members of my family and some of my carers, are also vegetarian, and some of them are against all kinds of animal products,

EXPERIMENTING WITH WEIGHT CONTROL

As I am unable to exercise, I find it very difficult to control my weight. As I have previously mentioned I am on the Slim Fast plan, having two Slim Fast meals a day and a balanced meal in the evening. I also use an ab-belt twice a day.

However, I recently started an alternative diet, which was recommended to me by my mother. The plan was to use this three days a week, and use my Slim Fast plan for another three days, leaving Sunday as my "free day." The diet consisted of meals such as poached egg on dry toast, half a grapefruit, cottage cheese and crackers and tuna on dry toast. I was only allowed to drink black coffee or water. The idea was that I would lose 40 pounds in month. I was told that this left me irritable and short tempered due to the drop in blood sugar caused by this diet. I tried it for a few weeks but decided to stop, as it was also leaving me very tired.

I also recently had problems with one of my ab-belts. I had been using this particular ab-belt for some time with adhesive pads, and had had no particular problem. I decided to try the plastic pads that were supplied with it, in conjunction with the conductive gel. I thought I would try this for a few weeks, but, after the first session, I had several burn marks on my stomach, even though I had used ample gel. I took photographs of these burn marks and sent them to the manufacturer, who requested that I return the ab-belt for inspection and a refund. I have done this and I am still waiting for a reply. I had previously taken it back to the shop as it had burnt me in the past, and after some dispute it was replaced. I am still interested in finding effective ways of losing weight, particularly around my stomach.

SURROUND SOUND

When I purchased my computer with the money that was raised in my Appeal, there was enough left over for me to be able to buy a surround sound, wide screen TV. This is ideal for my eyesight and gives full effect, just like being in a cinema. I recently had the speakers set up in my lounge by a friend who does this on a regular basis. It took him several hours to set up, but when it was finally installed the sound effects were astronomical. On some occasions the sounds make me jump as they come from different areas. I could never go back to a normal TV now that I have experienced this. The sound quality is also good when playing C.D's in my DVD player; it sounds even better than a normal hi-fi system. I have taken out an extra warranty and insurance for it.

USING THE INTERNET

After I received my computer I decided that I would get an Internet account, but I had never actually been on the Internet before. This is because it was still quite a new thing when I had my stroke. Now that I have got it I cannot be without it! It has opened up a whole new world for me. I am able to shop online and have things delivered to my door. I can find out an awful lot of information, especially on Only Fools and Horses products. In fact, anything that I need to know is available as soon as I log on. All that I want comes up on the screen. The best bit is that I don't have to book the van in advance or wait to go out, as it is all there ready for me. Using Email I am able to contact companies, organisations, family and friends and know that my message will get there instantly. I have even been into chat rooms with a carer, to get advice and technical support, which meant that I had a range of experts to hand immediately. I have un-metered access, and I only have to pay £15.99 a month by direct debit, and for this I get unlimited use, something that I don't get with the Treetops' van! The Internet can also tell me the best route to take when I am going on a journey, and the time it will take to get there.

RECEIVING MY VAN

On Monday 13th January 2003 I finally received my van, after a very long wait. When it arrived the carers were given a demonstration of how some of the things to do with the van are used. This included the tail lift, which is the platform that raises me and lowers me to the correct height, the clamps that secure the chair, the belts that strap me in and other things, like the heating, which will heat up, even if the engine is not running. This is very handy especially if I need to heat the van prior to going out. It is also beneficial as my body reacts to the surrounding temperature. We were even shown how the alarm system worked. It also came with tinted windows, which is very useful if I need private care within the van. It also makes the van very cool and trendy!

Since I have received my van I have been out quite a lot as new things are always a novelty at first and I have made good use of it. I have been to the Bluewater Shopping Centre in Kent and I have also had many shopping trips to Colchester and Ipswich, and I have felt very pleased with myself as several months ago I would never have dreamt of being this adventurous and independent, even within my own hometown. Now I can't keep away! It's surprising how much of Colchester has changed since I last saw it six years ago – before my stroke.

On other occasions it seems like it was only yesterday since I was last there, despite the changes. One other thing I would say is that I actually was trying to look around for people that I used to know. Whereas several months ago, I would never have dreamt of doing that as I was genuinely afraid of their reaction. So, I am quite pleased with how I have progressed. Now they can't keep me in!!!

STEPHEN AND PAULINE'S WEDDING

It was very enjoyable to see my brother Stephen back on the scene again, especially when he announced that he was engaged to a lady called Pauline.

Pauline has two girls from her previous marriage who are adorable.

Stephen still comes to see me regularly and Pauline and the girls visit when time allows.

Stephen and Pauline got married on the 23rd November 2002. I am really glad he now has a family and seems happy and settled.

The day of the wedding was a mixture of fun and emotion, most of the family was there as were Pauline's and everybody seemed to get on well together.

The wedding was held at Hedingham castle, which is very old and had very steep steps, so I was unable to get inside the castle itself for the ceremony, but I did actually have my photos taken outside with family members, which was still good.

The one thing that I did find funny about it is that I said, "It's a shame that they did not think of disabled access hundreds of years ago, how inconsiderate."

Pauline, her two girls and my niece, all wore saris and they looked quite beautiful.

Stephen was dressed in a black silk oriental outfit, he also had his nails painted black, which made him, look like a cross between fu-man-chu and someone who should be haunting the castle.

I did have a look for a rickshaw to see if he had arrived on one.

After the ceremony and the photo shoot, we all went off to the reception, which was held in the local village hall.

The road leading to the hall was very narrow for the bus to get down, so we all said if we breathe in we would be able to make it, which funnily enough we did, and it worked.

Overall it was a good day. There were a few tears when I had to leave. I hope they have a happy and healthy life together.

WHEN I MET DI

When I first went to Beckingham Court most of my laughs and conversations were with the night carers because I would let them know what I had been doing throughout the day, and all about any comical events which had occurred.

I mainly got on really well with one of these night carers called Di. She would be the one who would mainly look after me at night, so we were together for quite a lot of the time. I always felt as though there was something special between us, in a friendship way.

After being there a little while, one night I was just dozing off, when I felt a kiss on my cheek. I suddenly thought to myself, "Aye aye, I'm in here!" But, I didn't open my eyes to acknowledge it. Anyway, the following night when Di came to look after me, I said to her when there was no-one about, "Did you kiss me last night?" to which she said, "Yes I did, I hope you didn't mind."

I replied "On the contrary!" I then told her that I had grown special feelings towards her and she replied, " I feel the same way about you."

I suddenly thought to myself "This is a result!"

She then said to me " Would you mind if I could kiss you again." I replied "No, not at all."

This actually felt very nice because I hadn't experienced that for quite a while and I could actually feel my lips and also hers trembling. I think this was because we were so surprised at what we both felt for each other.

The following day I told my mother all about it and told her that we may well be "an item." She was so pleased to hear it that she gave me a big hug. After a little while Di got to know most of my family and I too got to know most of hers. She gradually became very good friends with Darren and Joy who used to stay round at Di's whenever they came down from Yorkshire to visit. We would quite often go out with Darren and Joy as a foursome, as well as me going round to Di's for the day so that we could be alone and together.

I eventually bought Di an eternity ring, which she would wear all of the time, which did make me feel really good and I enjoyed letting people know that we were an item. We would often get comments like " You are well suited," and, " You both seem to get on really well."

PORTRAIT OF DI AND ME

I have an uncle who is an artist and lives in Lowestoft, near Great Yarmouth. He recently contacted me and told me that he would love to do a portrait of Di and myself. I was very pleased with this idea and so was Di. He said that it would take several weeks to complete and that when it was finished he would bring it down to me personally. I eventually received a phone call from him, telling me that he had finished it and asking if he could come and see me. He arrived the following week and showed the portrait to me. I was very pleased with the result, as he had managed to leave out my tracheostomy and vent tube! He did a lovely job, and the portrait is now hanging in my lounge. He told me that he would be in touch again soon.

CARL AND DI

When I first started having a relationship with Di everything seemed to be perfect in every way, for example I would look forward to hearing from her by telephone, as it was really nice just to hear her voice. Most of the time she was committed to her work as a carer which did seem to take a lot of her time. I did understand this, as she told me she had quite a large mortgage and needed to work all of the hours under the sun to pay this. I did understand that visits from Di may be scarce so I made the most of enjoying our time when I did see her. The times that she could stay over was like winning the lottery because it was so nice being able to do normal things just like anybody else would. After a while I seemed to see Di on fewer occasions and getting Di to stay over was quite a task. I started to see Di hardly at all but I still treasured our telephone calls and it was still nice to hear her say that she still loved me. My brother Darren and his wife Joy used to come down from Yorkshire every few months to see the family and they would then stay at Di`s for a couple of days whilst they were down. What I did gradually seem to realise was that when Darren and Joy came down to stay at Di`s she was able to get time off work to be with them, but never with me. I tried not to think too much about it but I did mention it to Di on many occasions and she would make the excuse every time that she couldn't see me because of all the hours that she had to work. She would then say that when Darren and Joy did come down to stay it seemed to luckily be when she had time off work. It gradually became very difficult to get hold of Di even by telephone, so quite often I would leave a message but very rarely would she return my calls. I did start to think to myself, " I wonder if she is seeing someone else." I then thought to myself that I am being silly and then tried to put it to the back of my mind. I then began to realise that maybe I had guessed correctly, because every time I spoke to her she would say that she loved me, but these affectionate words seemed to fade, and I would rarely hear them from Di, but I would still say that I loved her. Then one day out of the blue, over four years into our relationship, she phoned me up and said that she didn't love me anymore and that it was over. I thought that she was joking but then she said it again and then I realised that she wasn't. I was very shocked and I tried to find out what I'd done wrong but all she kept saying was that I don't care for you anymore. She also ended her friendship with Darren and Joy, at which they too were very shocked. After I had spoken to Di on the telephone I tried not to let it show that I was upset so I kept it to myself for a couple of days which was very hard to do. Darren and Joy phoned me up quite upset, and they said that they didn't understand Di's change of feelings between myself and also with their friendship. I said to Darren and Joy that there must only be one reason for it, and that she must have met somebody else. When my mother found out she was very bitter and angry towards Di, she would try to get in contact with Di but on every occasion Di would avoid this. Then one morning, as mother was going to work,, she was arrested for causing harassment towards Di. Mother had a long interview with the police and explained to them all about me and how Di said she was very committed to our relationship. She did also say to Di at the time, are you quite sure that Carl is who you want, because if later on down the line, you decide to end the relationship and the family have to pick up the pieces due to me being hurt, then she could never forgive her. Di then said, " I know what I'm doing and I know that Carl is who I want." After mothers' long interview with the police they were very understanding, and realised why mother was trying to communicate with Di. They then released mother the same day with no charges.

MY VAN

Ever since I received my new Renault Master van through motability, it's done nothing but bring me bad luck. It has been hit on several occasions, not only when being driven, but even when parked in a car park somebody hit it and then drove off. It has been backwards and forwards to the main dealer quite a few times, and every time it comes back to me there is either something else wrong with it or the work, which it went in for, has not been done properly. It has also got a problem with the central locking that also occurred whilst being repaired. It seems to lock all the doors by itself, basically when it feels like it, which is quite a worry because one day it locked, and the window had to be smashed to get into the van, which is not really ideal. It has also got wet on the inside on a few occasions where the rain has leaked through the doors where they weren't refitted properly. At first it was a mystery as the van seats, curtains and carpets would be wet the following day after rain, which we could not understand. I do hope that my van does get restored to its original condition because when it goes in for repair I really do miss having the use of it.

DAY TRIP TO FRANCE

Ever since I've had my van I have always wanted, if it was at all possible, to go to somewhere like France for the day. I was told that this may be possible, but it would have to be looked into properly before going. I was so pleased to hear that I could go, so I decided to make a list of things to look out for, for example, alcohol!

The day that I left for France I had to make sure everything I needed was in order, and also that I was ready on time to leave. When we left to go to Folkestone for the Euro Tunnel we had to leave early to avoid traffic. When we arrived at Folkestone to get onto the train I was a little apprehensive about a few things. For example, my passport photograph didn't really look identical to me because I had the photo taken quite a few years ago, but they let me through with no problems. I also wondered how the carers would get on driving in France, as the French drive on the opposite side of the road to what we do in this country. They managed it really well, but I was still confused, especially when approaching roundabouts.

Another concern which I did have, was that if my conveen decided to leak, how would I go about changing. I tried not to think about that happening but, as soon as I got into France my bad luck came true and my conveen decided to leak! As you can imagine, I was so overwhelmed and had a few choice words to say, but it was a choice of either going back home, or changing the conveen in the toilets to make myself as comfortable as possible. I said that I was not going to come all this way and then have to go straight back again, so I put a big smile on my face and carried on around France.

There was one thing that felt really strange, and that was when we went through the tunnel my ears blocked, just like on an airplane, so I sucked on a sweet, which was supposed to help unblock my ears. They did unblock a little, but my full hearing didn't really return until I was back home in bed, because the same thing happened on the journey home.

ACTIVITIES AT TREETOPS NURSING HOME

Even though I am in my own home, I am still able to be involved with any events that may arise at Treetops. I sometimes visit Treetops if the weather is nice as I know many of the residents and staff, and it is nice to keep in touch.

Quite recently, they celebrated the Queen's Golden Jubilee, and had many stalls and activities going on throughout the day and into the evening. They also had a mini auction and one of the items that was up for auction was an autographed Colchester United football T-Shirt, which was signed by all the players, which luckily I won the bid for. I have now put the shirt alongside my autographed jockey trousers, signed by all of the jockeys at Ascot, and my signed photograph of Ipswich Town Football Club, signed by the Chairman. I do intend to attend more of Treetops' functions as I feel very welcome there.

One way in which I can keep an eye on my weight, is by the same means as at Stoke Mandeville. Treetops have platform scales. First of all you weigh the wheelchair, and then myself in the wheelchair and then subtract the wheelchair weight from the total weight. I am really glad that Treetops have this facility, as it means I am able to keep track of my weight. I don't have to wait for an appointment at Stoke Mandeville, as previously that was the only place where I could get weighed.

I SEEM TO BE INVISIBLE

One thing that I have noticed since my rehabilitation to leading a normal life is that people who's path I cross, seem to direct questions to whoever is with me e.g. my carer, instead of talking to me. Often I have found that when I am out I am stared at, or people sigh and smile, as if in pity. There have been those I have come across who ask questions relating to myself, to my carer, even though I can talk, hear and communicate very well with others. It is automatically assumed that I am incapable of holding a conversation.

Those who approach my carer or family will ask, "How old is he?" " What happened to him?" "Can he talk?" This is while I am sitting there, often thinking, "Hello, I'm here!"

Most of the time I will chuckle to myself and think how silly people can be, but other times it upsets me. After all, I am a human being and have feelings, but I try to get used to it as I know that it will always happen unless I fit in socially. I am an outcast because of my disability. Unless I carry a sign round with me that states I can talk, people will always make assumptions, I do not blame people for this, as it is human nature, most do not know how to react to me.

I would also like to mention that I find it highly rude when people talk over me, walk into me (which happens often), it is like being a child again, when the adults talk the child must be quiet, only I am not a child.

This is one of the reasons I have called this section 'I seem to be invisible', but I would like to mention there are those who are very considerate and friendly, who do treat me like everyone else, which ultimately is what I want. There are those who will open doors for me and ask how I am, directly. I do not consider this special treatment, merely good manners. In these circumstances it would be easy for me to take advantage, if I wanted something, but I don't. I appreciate good manners and politeness, this is far more important to me than what I can get for myself.

There are many areas that I feel anger or frustration about in regards to other people and how they react to me. I do however understand the difficulty some people have as there isn't enough awareness to a disabled persons needs and emotional needs. Someone answering for me for instance, I find most offensive, as again it re-affirms that to some people I do not exist. There have been a few times in restaurants, where the waiter/waitress will ask the carer what I would like. I will respond with, "I would like!!" Some people are taken back by this. There have also been some carers that act in the same way. They will bend down, look at me straight in the face and shout, "Are you alright." (Which has become a bit of a joke). There have been some carers who have dipped their finger in my drink to see if it is too hot for me; would you like that? Also some who have cut up my food and then blown on it to cool it for me!!!! To me, this is treating me like a child, not an adult, and showing little to no respect for me or my feelings at all, even if the carer only wishes to be nice by doing these things for me. On a quick note, I would like to mention how nice it is when I phone someone, like a bank or a retail outlet. They do not see the person on the other end of the phone, they are unaware that I am disabled and on a ventilator, they treat me like a customer, the average Joe, which is all I want from anybody.

ANNUAL TRIP TO STOKE MANDEVILLE

In February 2003 I had my annual check up at Stoke Mandeville hospital, where they give you a full check up which I call my M O T.

I had several tests which cover most areas of my care e.g. weight, tracheal care, bladder, bowels and medication. It was a very long day.

I went there in my new van with three of my carers. Mother and Di met me there. I was so pleased that they were there to give me support, because I was nervous enough already. I was so anxious about having all the tests done, even though I have had all of them before. I suppose I was anxious because I didn't know what they might find.

Leading up to the appointment I was getting very tearful, the reason being is that I was trying not to think about when I eventually go into hospital regarding my kidney stones. Everything about the operation was going around in my head and I kept asking myself the same questions.

   i.   Who is going to look after me?

   ii. How long will it all take?

   iii. How long will I be there?

   iv. Will I make it through the operation?

These were all negative thoughts.

After I had had all of the tests we had to meet the Consultant who explained it all to us, they looked at my x-rays and also previous x-rays.

He basically told me that I was in a very good condition and that he couldn't find any problems. After he had spoken to us he said that he would send on all of my results in writing, through the post. He more or less said, I will see you in a year.

Overall I was quite pleased with the result and a lot of my anxiety went after speaking to him

After seeing the consultant we went for a bite to eat in the hospital canteen and to chat about the tests that I had. We then visited the ward that I had stayed in for 3 years while I was there. I saw a lot of the nurses, which I knew from the past. We had a general chat with them and they were interested in what I had been up to. They seemed pleased to see me and commented on how well I was looking.

I eventually left for home. I did remember the Consultant said to me that my kidney stones had hardly increased in size at all. He also said for the time being we will just keep an eye on them.

Several weeks later I received a letter saying that they don't know how, but for some reason, the kidney stone obstruction seemed to have disappeared, which naturally I thought was some kind of joke. I then said how could this be possible, everybody was confused and bewildered but also very pleased and overjoyed. I could not believe what I was hearing. I then thought to myself could this have happened because of my exercise belt, which vibrates on my stomach. When I first started using it I had a lot of blood pass through my urine, as well as fragments, like grit. So, what could have happened is that my exercise belt may have dislodged them, so I could have passed them naturally.

I am glad with how everything has turned out and I can now get on with my life, hopefully stress free!

New home for stroke victim?

Hope tragic Carl could return to Colchester soon

by SHARON ASPLIN

A STROKE victim whose family is battling to have him treated near Colchester could be offered a home in the area — thanks to the County Standard.

About two and a half years ago Carl Holmes, now 25, had a stroke while weightlifting at his cousin's home.

He is now on a ventilator, registered blind and needs two full-time carers 24 hours a day.

Mr Holmes, a former Sir Charles Lucas pupil who lived at Tippett Close, Colchester, is currently receiving specialist care in Stoke Mandeville Hospital.

But his stepfather Martin Buxton and mother Doreen have been trying to obtain a home for him near Colchester, backed with a full care package.

And yesterday Mr Buxton confirmed a home in the Colchester area, which had seen the original story of Carl's plight in the Standard, had been in touch.

"Obviously it is early days yet," he said.

BATTLING ON — stroke victim Carl Holmes, pictured before the tragedy, could be moved nearer to Colchester.

"We have visited the place and Carl seems quite keen but there are a number of things we need to look at regarding the details of the care package he will receive, his social needs and funding.

"Certainly it is more hopeful and I hope things can be arranged fairly quickly. At the moment Carl is in hospital just wasting away."

Negotiations are now ongoing between Mr Holmes and his parents, the home and Essex Rivers Healthcare Trust.

Mr Buxton hopes Colchester MP Bob Russell will attend a meeting due to be held shortly to give the family support.

The trust has described Mr Holmes' case as "extremely tragic, unusual and complicated" but said the health authority was prepared to pay for whatever care was appropriate.

Del Boy is luvverly jubberly for visiting

IT was a visit, not by Santa, but by actor David Jason which really made Christmas that bit special for 26-year-old stroke victim Carl Holmes.

Carl, who comes from Essex, suffered a stroke three years ago and is currently in Stoke Mandeville Hospital.

In the summer he was visited in hospital by the Only Fools and Horses star, after staff heard Carl was a fan of the TV series and arranged a meeting with the actor, who lives at Ellesborough.

Carl's mum, Doreen Buxton, said: "Since then he has never forgotten Carl and has sent him messages of support and birthday cards.

But then, on Christmas Eve, Del Boy, as he is known by Carl, paid an unexpected visit and spent a long time chatting to him.

"David Jason is absolutely fantastic and his visits and messages mean so much to Carl, who is on a ventilator 24 hours a day," said Doreen.

It is hoped that in February Carl can be moved to a hospital closer to his home.

"Before he left on Friday David told him that, even when he was moved, he would still come to visit him," she said.

KIND: David Jason

CHAT: Carl Holmes

TODAY the Essex County Standard launches a special appeal to help a young Colchester stroke victim who has finally come home.

Three years ago Carl Holmes, 26, suffered a massive stroke while weight training at his cousin's home.

It left him so ill his family was warned he would probably not survive.

But, although now paralysed and needing 24-hour care, Carl has proved to be a fighter.

Inside we reveal his battle against the odds and ask you, our readers, to help his family's quest to improve his quality of life by providing him with a voice-activated computer.

And in a heart-felt message to County Standard readers, Carl said: "A computer will make a great difference to my life.

"Although I cannot get a job like any other normal able-bodied person, I have an ambition to further my career and if I am lucky enough to get a kind sponsor who can help me with a computer then I would love to do my own stationery business."

The County Standard has always taken Carl's plight to its heart.

When his distraught family were told the only option was to send him to the south of the country for treatment, away from all his loved ones, we stepped in to run an appeal in the paper.

● **Continued on page two**
● **Coming home – Carl's full story see special report on pages 32 and 33**

TV David's mercy trip

By AIDAN McGURRAN

TV star David Jason has taken time off to cheer up a fan who suffered a devastating stroke.

The actor, who plays Inspector Frost, lives near Stoke Mandeville hospital, Bucks, and was asked by staff to cheer up Carl Holmes, 25, who is registered blind and on a ventilator after being struck down while weight training.

His mum Doreen said yesterday: "David was so kind. He stayed an hour, cuddled Carl and promised to go back again."

FLASHBACKS – how the County Standard helped highlight Carl's plight. Left: February 3, 1999. Above: August 13, 1999.

County Standard campaigned for move

THE County Standard has been at the forefront of the fight to bring Carl home.

Back in March 1999 we ran an appeal for help to find him somewhere to live in the Colchester area, somewhere that could care for his needs but at the same time provide the right environment for him to be happy.

His family were distraught when it seemed the only suitable care for him would be somewhere in the south of England, even further away from them than Stoke Mandeville Hospital.

But management at Beckingham Court rehabilitation unit in Tolleshunt Major came forward when they saw his appeal in the County Standard offering him a home.

Even then it was not straightforward. Complicated negotiations had to be carried out between the various health authorities, the family and the home to ensure everything was suitable for him.

But the waiting paid off and his care will be paid for by North Essex Health Authority.

Doreen cannot wait until Carl is safely in Tolleshunt Major. Instead of a long drive away, he will be just be 15 minutes from her home.

She said: "I just want to thank the Essex County Standard for making this possible. They were the only ones at that time who seemed to be listening."

Association

● THE Stroke Association is a national charity which provides practical support to people who have had strokes and their families and carers.

● It campaigns, educates and informs to increase knowledge of stroke at all levels of society.

● The association also runs telephone helplines, provides publications and welfare grants. Volunteers also work to improve communication skills with people who have lost the ability to speak, read or write.

● Although it works closely with health authorities, policy makers and other bodies to ensure stroke victims have access to the best possible treatment and care, the association relies almost entirely on the generosity of the general public.

We are here to help Carl

A LOCAL charity has pledged to give Carl and his family all the support they need when he moves back to the Colchester area next week.

The Stroke Association has urged them to get in touch if they have any questions at all about his condition.

Ann Condie, the association's regional manager for East Anglia, said: "It is a very cruel illness.

"Because people can have communication difficulties as well as physical problems people who do not understand about stroke – and often that includes the family – do not realise the person's intellect is locked inside a body which no longer obeys them.

"That can be incredibly frustrating for everyone."

She explained that unlike some other illnesses, stroke was not deteriorating and the victim could live a normal lifespan with the disabilities it had caused.

The association is always in need of funds to continue to help stroke victims and their families.

If anyone can help contact 01394 279933.

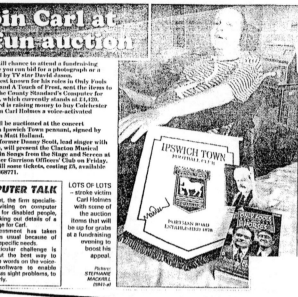

Join Carl at a fun auction

THERE is still chance to attend a fundraising event where you can bid for a photograph or a video signed by TV star David Jason.

The actor, best known for his roles in Only Fools and Horses and A Touch of Frost, sent the items to help boost the County Standard's Computer for Carl Appeal, which currently stands at £4,420.

The Standard is raising money to buy Colchester stroke victim Carl Holmes a voice-activated computer.

The gifts will be auctioned at the concert alongside an Ipswich Town pennant, signed by team captain Matt Holland.

Popular performer Danny Scott, lead singer with The Beavers, will present the Clacton Musical Performers in Songs from the Stage and Screen at the Colchester Garrison Officers' Club on Friday.

There are still some tickets, costing £5, available from 01206 868771.

COMPUTER TALK

ABILITY Net, the firm specialising in advising on computer equipment for disabled people, is still working out details of a final package for Carl.

The assessment has taken longer than usual because of Carl's very specific needs.

The particular challenge is working out the best way to magnify the words on the voice-activated software to enable Carl, who has sight problems, to view it clearly.

LOTS OF LOTS – stroke victim Carl Holmes with some of the auction items that will be up for grabs at a fundraising evening to boost his appeal.

Picture: STEPHANIE MACKRILL (5941-a)

Support for stroke victim's fight to return to Essex

Battle for Carl to move home

by JENNY ANDREWS

HOSPITAL consultants are to join the fight to get a young stroke victim treated closer to home.

Carl Holmes, 25, who lived in Tippetts Close, Colchester, has spent the last 18 months at Stoke Mandeville Hospital in Buckinghamshire.

The stroke, which happened about two and a half years ago, has left him paralysed from the neck down.

Stepfather Martin Buxton and mother Doreen, of Chelmsford, have been battling to obtain a home for him in Colchester backed up with a full care package.

But Essex Rivers Healthcare Trust feel medically Mr Holmes is not ready for such a move and have secured a place for him in a care home in Guildford.

Now his consultants are to write to the Trust recommending he should be able to live in the community with a care package.

Mr Buxton said: "His consultants think he would have a better chance living in the community. Medical opinions should carry some weight and we have been told by one of the consultants that Carl's life expectancy would be better served by him going back into the community.

QUALITY

"He would have a better quality of life. He has been in hospital 18 months longer than he should have been and it is not good enough."

The family have also an appointment to see Colchester MP Bob Russell who said today: "I or the family's constituency MP will do everything we can to make representations on their behalf."

Former ambulance makes ideal wheels for stroke victim

Carl Holmes, pictured with Claire Graham at Tolleshunt Major, now has wheels.   8539-0

STROKE victim Carl Holmes has a new set of wheels.

Carl, who is a resident at Beckingham Court rehabilitation unit in Tolleshunt Major, has been looking for a vehicle which can carry both him and his ventilator.

And now he is the proud owner of a former ambulance.

Wrights Vehicle Sales on Canvey Island read about Carl's plight in our sister paper the Essex County Standard and offered to knock £500 off the price of the vehicle.

One of Carl's relatives then came up with the £1,000 needed to buy the ambulance and other members of the family are now raising money to pay them back.

The 26-year-old was left paralysed after he suffered a massive stroke three years ago while weight-training at his cousin's house.

Carl was so ill that doctors warned his family that he might not survive.

But, although he is now paralysed and needs a ventilator and 24-hour care, Carl has fought back.

He is slowly regaining his sight, ability to eat and drink and his speech.

Officer wanted to raise cash

THE Chelmsford and Mid-Essex branch of the Samaritans is appealing for a fund raising officer to boost resources.

The voluntary post would suit someone who has a few hours to spare a week, but does not have to work as a full time Samaritan.

...year to operate successfully and gets no grant aid.

The volunteer would complement the work of the Friends of the Samaritans not just raising money to run the branch, but also to reach out to its catchment area of Maldon, Witham, Braintree and Great Dunmow.

The branch needs £90,000 ● Contact 01245 357357.

Farmers' market a step nearer

Terry and Mike's slimline tonic for Carl appeal

by SHARON ASPLIN

CONGRATULATIONS — our super slimmers have done it!

Two months ago Colchester councillor Terry Sutton and Essex County Newspapers' sub-editor Mike Chaplin embarked on a sponsored slim for the County Standard Computer for Carl Appeal.

Both set themselves targets and both have come through the ordeal with flying colours — not to mention boosting our appeal to the tune of £547.

Mr. Sutton, Colchester Council deputy leader and borough Liberal Democrat councillor for Borechurch, tipped the scales at the beginning of March at 18 stone 12 pounds.

He aimed to lose two stones but has finally weighed in at 16 stone and 9 pounds. He pledged £5 for every pound he shed and with this and other sponsorship, has raised £420.

He said this week: "I feel a lot healthier and fitter and I would like to lose some more.

"But now I have got to buy some more clothes — I have lost three inches from my waist and am having to use braces to hold my trousers up. It was great to do something for my own health as well as for Carl and everyone, especially...

STANDARD COMPUTER FOR CARL APPEAL

Slimming World, has given me a huge amount of encouragement.

Mr. Chaplin, now a svelte 12 stones down from 13 stones, is also keen to lose some more weight.

He had pledged to lose a stone and did so by eating sensibly and increasing his exercise.

He has raised £127.

"I'm glad Carl gave me the inspiration to do this," he said. "I'm glad I helped him as well as myself. I'm continuing on the diet and plan to lose a further half stone — I'm not finished yet."

● When collected, the £547 will go towards the appeal to buy Colchester stroke victim Carl Holmes a voice-activated computer. The appeal currently stands at £3,097.

● The County Standard boosts the appeal — see centre pages.

SUPER SLIMMER — a slimline Terry Sutton is congratulated on losing two stone and three pounds by the members of Slimming World at the Arena Leisure Centre who supported him all the way.

Picture:
NIGEL BROWN
(8644-2)

FLASHBACK — Terry Sutton and Mike Chaplin, pictured left, find out the dreaded truth as they weighed in two months ago.

HOW YOU CAN HELP

YOU can also send a donation or arrange a fund raising event on Carl's behalf, contact reporter Sharon Asplin on 01206 506277 or send a donation to:

Computer for Carl Appeal, Essex County Standard, Oriel House, 43 North Hill, Colchester, CO1 1TZ, or take it to Barclays Bank, High Street, Colchester, and ask for the Computer for Carl Appeal, sort number 20-22-69, account number 00230332.

Cheques should be made payable to Computer for Carl Appeal.

SNOOKER

Stroke victim Carl is coming home

by SHARON ASPLIN

A COLCHESTER stroke victim will finally come home in the new year.

Carl Holmes, who suffered a stroke three years ago this week, has been receiving treatment in Stoke Mandeville Hospital but his family have been fighting for months to have him transferred closer to home.

And they confirmed this week he will be moved to a rehabilitation unit in Tolleshunt Major on February 29.

His delighted mother Doreen Buxton said: "We are just so thrilled we are all going to be nearer him. It will make it so much easier to visit.

Carl had the stroke while he was weightlifting. He is now paralysed and needs 24-hour a day care.

Staff at Beckenham Court came forward to offer Carl a place after reading an appeal by his family in the County Standard earlier this year.

And it is a double celebration for Carl this week who became an uncle for the first time.

On Tuesday his brother Darren and sister-in-law Joy became the proud parents of baby Juliet.

Darren Holmes, a mathematics teacher at Sir Charles Lucas School, met his wife while she was nursing Carl at Stoke Mandeville and proposed by his bedside.

Surprise visitor for brave stroke victim Carl

by LESLEY HEUER

COLCHESTER stroke victim Carl Holmes had a special Christmas Eve visitor.

Top TV actor David Jason popped into Stoke Mandeville Hospital, where Carl has been receiving treatment, to personally deliver a Christmas card and spend some time talking to him.

It was the second time 25-year-old Carl has received a visit from his favourite television star (pictured).

And it came just a few weeks before his planned move to a rehabilitation unit at Beckenham Court in Tolleshunt Major.

Carl's mother, Doreen Buxton, said: "When David saw him he asked Carl about his move, and said he would come to see him once he was settled in.

"His first words to Carl were 'Blimey mate you've lost some weight!' – Carl has been on a diet and has managed to lose two stones since the summer."

Carl suffered a stroke while weightlifting three years ago. He is now paralysed and in need of 24-hour care. He is due to make the move back to Essex on February 29.

Del's tonic for Carl

by Jeni Connibeer

STOKE Mandeville Hospital can now be added to the Nag's Head, Peckham High Street, and Nelson Mandela House as hang outs of lovable rogue Del Boy after he made a surprise appearance on one of the wards.

The popular actor, David Jason, turned up unexpectedly to visit stroke victim and only Fools and Horses fan Carl Holmes in the spinal injuries unit. And the 25-year-old, who has been at Stoke for more than two years, was over the moon to see the hero of his favourite TV show.

"I was quoting bits at him and he said I knew them better than he did," said Carl who couldn't believe what he was seeing when David Jason appeared at his bedside. He stayed for about an hour and a half and he had a lady friend with him. She was lovely, her name was Jill.

"When they left I called David a plonker and he turned around and said I was a dipstick. It was the best thing that ever happened to me."

Carl suffered a stroke three years ago which left him paralysed, unable to speak and partially blind. Now he can talk and his sight is returning but he still needs 24-hour care.

Recently Carl, who is from Colchester, had become increasingly depressed about his situation and staff at the hospital decided to try to get his hero to pay him a visit.

The devoted nurses, who somehow arranged the celebrity visit, are remaining mysterious about how they managed to get Del Boy on board but the effect he had is not hard to see.

"He just arrived and said he had come to cheer me up," said Carl, and his mum,' Doreen, added the visit had done wonders. "He was so overwhelmed he just started crying," she said. "So did I when he told me all about it."

SURPRISE: David Jason, left, visited Carl, above, in hospital

Letter boost for Carl

by SHARON ASPLIN

TV star David Jason, whose visit brightened the day of a Colchester stroke victim, has now dropped him a line in a bid to cheer him up again.

The Only Fools and Horses star popped in to see Carl Holmes, 25, in Stoke Mandeville Hospital after nurses noticed he was getting very depressed by his condition.

Mr Jason wrote: "Just thought I would drop you a line to say that it was good to see you the other week and I hope that you have watched the tape and read the book that I bought. Questions will be asked later, so get swotting.

"If ever I am passing with some free time, I'll pop in again and have another cup of tea with you."

In true Del Boy style he has signed off: "Bonjour, David Jason".

Mr Holmes had a stroke while weightlifting nearly three years ago. He is now paralysed and needs 24-hour a day care.

It is hoped he will be transferred to a rehabilitation unit in Tolleshunt Major by the end of the year to be nearer his family.

HERO — Only Fools and Horses star David Jason chats to Carl Holmes.

17th August, 1998

David Jason

Carl Holmes,
St. Andrews Ward,
National Spinal Injuries Centre,
Stoke Mandeville Hospital,
Mandeville Road,
Aylesbury,
Buckinghamshire,
HP21 8AL.

Dear Carl,

Just thought I would drop you a line to say that it was good to see you the other week and I hope that you have watched the tape and read the book that I bought. Questions will be asked later, so get swotting.

If ever I am passing with some free time, I'll pop in again and have another cup of

CARING — part of David Jason's letter to Carl.

ESSEX COUNTY STANDARD

HELP GIVE CARL A VOICE

HOW WE HELPED

LEFT: – how we launched the appeal in last week's Essex County Standard.

Dancers – get in line for Carl!

DANCERS are being asked to get in line for Carl.

Kathy Kibble, who is a close family friend, is organising a line dance on Friday, May 5.

All proceeds will go to the Computer for Carl Appeal.

Mrs Kibble said: "Our families have always been very close and I thought this would be a great idea to raise some money."

The event will be at the Queens Hall, Halstead, and generous caller Kym Barry from the Halstead Grapeviners is giving her services free of charge.

Tickets are £5 each. For details and to book call Mrs Kibble on 01787 475621 or Kym Barry on 01787 476508.

> ENTERTAINER Bill Carter has offered his services to the Computer for Carl Appeal. One-man band Bill from Brightlingsea says he will provide 50s and 60s music, free of charge, to anyone wishing to organise a fundraising event for Carl. Call him on 01206 307004.

TV David's mercy trip

By AIDAN McGURRAN

TV star David Jason has taken time off to cheer up a fan who suffered a devastating stroke.

The actor, who plays Inspector Frost, lives near Stoke Mandeville hospital, Bucks, and was asked by staff to cheer up Carl Holmes, 25, who is registered blind and on a ventilator after being struck down while weight training.

His mum Doreen said yesterday: "David was so kind. He stayed an hour, cuddled Carl and promised to go back again."

A touch of Frost aid

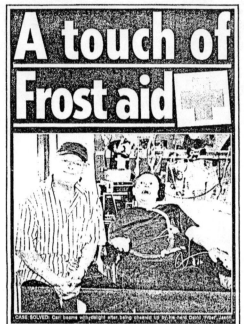

CASE SOLVED: Carl beams with delight after being cheered up by his hero David 'Frost' Jason

IT was an open and shut case when crusty telly detective Jack Frost was asked to cheer up a sick fan.

The tough-talking cop—alias actor David Jason—immediately took time out from his busy schedule to investigate why Carl Holmes was down in the dumps at Stoke Mandeville Hospital.

Carl, 26, has battled back from the brink of death since being paralysed by a stroke three years ago. But the weight lifter, from Chelmsford, Essex, had spiralled into a deep depression over his painfully slow rate of recovery.

Caring

So when caring nurses at the world famous hospital in Aylesbury, Bucks, discovered Carl had been a fan of David ever since he first appeared as Del Boy in Only Fools And Horses, they asked the star to drop him a line.

But kind-hearted David—who lost the love of his life, Myfanwy Talog, to cancer five years ago at the same hospital—went one better and instead paid Carl a visit.

Stunned Carl revealed: "I recognised him instantly but couldn't believe my eyes. He walked up to

Star David's get Del soon wish for fan

BY VANESSA LARGE

my bed and said 'Hello Carl, I've come to cheer you up'.

"And he was as good as his word. He sat and chatted with me for an hour over a cup of tea. It was like we were old friends.

"He brought me an Only Fools And Horses book and video. We laughed about Del Boy's antics and I told him my favourite moments from the series.

"I have watched it so often I can recite virtually all of it off by heart. David joked that I was after his job but no one could take his place he's the greatest."

Carl added: "There was a time when I felt sorry for myself and depressed—but I don't feel sorry any more. David's friendship makes me feel very privileged, very special and very lucky."

As well as his lead roles in Only Fools And Horses and A Touch Of Frost, David played Granville alongside Ronnie Barker's domineering Arkwright in Open All Hours, which pulled in 18.9 mil-

lion viewers for the BBC at its peak in 1985. Better still was the Only Fools And Horses Christmas special when Del won the lottery, which drew 24 million viewers.

And when David switched to ITV to play Pa Larkin in the Darling Buds Of May, every episode topped the ratings, peaking at 18.34 million viewers.

But fame hasn't gone to his head and he certainly hasn't forgotten his fans. Since he first visited Carl in September, the star has sent his new pal a birthday card and popped in over Christmas to check he's still smiling.

Carl's mum, Doreen Buxton, said: "I can't believe what David has done for my son.

"He's given him a reason to live again. Carl has had such a hard time and the depression sent him in a downward spiral. David's visit really picked him up and made him feel very special."

Grateful

"I want to thank him for the kindness he has shown my son. I want him to know the difference he has made to Carl and tell him how grateful we are. Despite his fame he's still very down to earth—that's why he's so popular."

But modest David, who has found new happiness with TV girl Gill Hinchliffe since Myfanwy's death, reckons HE had been inspired by CARL.

He said: "I've been really impressed by Carl and wish him well for the future."

Our View: Page 18

176

David Jason

17th August, 1999

Carl Holmes,
St. Andrews Ward,
National Spinal Injuries Centre,
Stoke Mandeville Hospital,
Mandeville Road,
Aylesbury,
Buckinghamshire,
HP21 8AL.

Dear Carl,

Just thought I would drop you a line to say that it was good to see you the other week and I hope that you have watched the tape and read the book that I brought. Questions will be asked later, so get swotting.

If ever I am passing with some free time, I'll pop in again and have another cup of tea with you. So don't forget to keep some nice biccies on stand by.

Regards to you and your ward.

Bonjour,

David Jason

DAVID JASON

8th August, 2000

Carl Holmes,
Beckingham Court,
Brickhouse Lane,
Toleshunt Major,
Essex,   CM9 8JX.

Dear Carl,

Thank you for your recent letter. I am pleased to hear that you are continuing to settle in well in your new home. What's all this about an autobiography? You'll be appearing on "Parkinson" next or "Richard and Judy"!

Glad to hear that your weight loss programme was such a success. I am sure that it will be better for you but I agree you should have a sin day on Sundays. Lots of lovely roast beef and Yorkshire Puddings – luvly jubbly!

I hope you haven't got your new bar stocked up with booze in Beckingham Court, especially if you drink Del Boy style cocktails. Mind you, I hope you're not going to start smoking cigars or they really will think about transferring you back to Stoke Mandeville.

Anyway Carl, just thought I would write this short note between my filming days on "Frost" which takes me backwards and forwards to Yorkshire as you know. Gill comes up when she can and helps point me in the right direction.

Take care,

David Jason

Dear Carl,

I was very pleased to hear from you as I had mislaid your new address since your move from Stoke Mandeville for which I apologise.

You certainly seem to be enjoying your new surroundings and friends and it must be great for you to be getting out and about. We'll have to look out for a second-hand ambulance bombing about. Why didn't you get a yellow three-wheeler?!!!

I am glad that you've enjoyed reading "David Jason – In His Element". Now you know what I get up to when I'm filming. That particular project took place last year and I was out of the country for at least three weeks. Very soon, I'll be off to Yorkshire to film another special of "A Touch of Frost". I should know every lump and bump of the M1 by now, the number of times I have been backwards and forwards to Leeds.

I agree with Sir Jimmy Saville that you are getting more publicity than the two of us put together. We'll be having to call you "Sir" soon.

Gill is very well and sends you her best wishes. We are both pleased to hear that you have settled in so well to Beckingham Court and hope that you go from strength to strength.

On that note, I will wish you all the best for the moment as I have to buckle down to a big mountain of paperwork. Just before I go, I'm pleased to hear that you're still watching the videos – you know it makes sense.

Au revoir

P.S. Don't forget – he who dares wins!

Donations bring voice computer purchase closer

AND still it keeps pouring in.

This week the County Standard Computer for Carl Appeal has smashed the £2,000 barrier – with the grand total yesterday standing at a magnificent £2,245.

A marvellous £975 in cheques was delivered to the County Standard offices and Barclays Bank this week.

This means we are almost on the verge of being able to provide Carl with the voice-activated computer he needs.

Acting County Standard editor Neal Hurrington said: "The response from our caring readers has been amazing. The compassion shown to Carl's appeal is quite inspirational.

"The computer will make a significant difference to Carl's quality of life. Well done County Standard readers and please keep up the good work!"

Carl's mum Doreen Buxton said she was absolutely delighted with the success of the appeal.

She said: "I'm just over the moon, everybody has been so kind and thoughtful, we are just thrilled to bits that people out there do care.

"At the moment there are so many other tragedies across the world, like Mozambique, and it is nice that people are still being so generous to Carl.

"And once again, all praise to the Essex County Standard – we could not have done it without you."

Three years ago Carl suffered a massive stroke while weight training at his cousin's home.

PARALYSED

It left him so ill his family was warned he would not probably not survive.

But, although now paralysed and needing a ventilator and 24-hour care, Carl has fought back, slowly regaining his sight, ability to eat and drink and his speech.

The County Standard launched the Computer for Carl Appeal to provide him with a voice-activated computer to improve his quality of life.

CAN HELP

TO send a donation or arrange a fundraising event on Carl's behalf, contact reporter Sharon Asplin on 01206 508277 or send a donation to: *Computer for Carl* Appeal, Essex County Standard, Oriel House, 43 North Hill, Colchester, CO1 1TZ, or take it to Barclays Bank, High Street, Colchester, and ask for the Computer for Carl Appeal, sort number 20-22-69, account number 00230332.

Cheques should be made payable to Computer for Carl Appeal.

ESSE ST

FRIDAY, AUGUST 27, 1999

Bonjour Carl, says Del Boy

David Jason visit — p3

The software recommended by the experts to make it voice activated is Dragon Naturally Speaking Professional, costing £450. This is very powerful and would give Carl a high level of independence.

Installation and full training to adapt the computer for Carl's exact needs would cost another £500.

● See our front page for details of how to make a donation to Carl's appeal.

Big game special as Wrighty heads for Layer Road
U's news on page 59

Millennium town spotlight falls on The Hythe
PAGE 16

The town's top guide to property
40-page pullout

HELP GIVE CARL A VOICE

Carl Holmes

by SHARON ASPLIN

TODAY the Essex County Standard launches a special appeal to help a young Colchester stroke victim who has finally come home.

Three years ago Carl Holmes, 26, suffered a massive stroke while weight training at his cousin's home.

It left him so ill his family was warned he would probably not survive.

Touch of spring down on the farm

THE sight of lambs gambolling in the fields and farmyard is always a sign that winter is almost over and spring is on the way.

On Sunday, Peldon farmers Liz and Robert Davidson will be holding their annual Lamb Watch to help raise money for the restoration of St Mary's church in Peldon.

If you go along to Brickhouse Farm, Lower Road, Peldon, between 1pm and 4pm you will be able to see some of the hundreds of lambs born since the end of January.

There may even be a chance to see new-born lambs taking their first tottering steps. Visitors can stroke

01206 508277 or send a donation to: Computer for Carl, Essex County Standard, Oriel House, 43 North Hill, Colchester, CO1 1TZ, or take them to Barclays Bank, High Street, Colchester, and ask for Computer for Carl Appeal, sort number 20-22-69, account number 00230332.

fighter.

Inside we reveal his battle against the odds and ask you, our readers, to help his family's quest to improve his quality of life by providing him with a second-hand computer.

And in a heart-felt message to County Standard readers, Carl said: "A computer will make a great difference to my life.

"Although I cannot get a job like any other normal able-bodied person, I have an ambition to further my career and if I am lucky enough to get a kind sponsor who can help me with a computer then I would love to do my own stationery business."

The County Standard has always taken Carl's plight to its heart.

When his distraught family were told the only option was to send him to the south of the country for treatment, away from all his loved ones, we stepped in to run an appeal in the paper.

● Continued on page two
● Coming home – Carl's full story see special report on pages 32 and 33

Admission is £4 per car, and there is plenty of parking available.

LITTLE LAMB – Amy Swinton, 8, cuddles up to one of the new-born lambs at Brickhouse Farm, Peldon.
Picture: STEVE ARGENT (7552-4)

Armed raider strikes twice

BRAVE shopkeepers fought off an armed robber who attacked two Colchester stores within the space of an hour.

In the first raid, at Winnock Road sub-post office in New Town on Wednesday, a raider armed with an iron bar threatened the sub-postmaster and his son.

But instead of handing over the cash as he demanded, they grappled with him in an attempt to restrain him until police arrived.

Det Sgt Roger Napier, of Colchester police, said: "They had a tussle with this robber and at one stage managed to pin him to

the ground. But he escaped and ran off."

The sub-postmaster's son chased the raider and caught up with him a short way down the street.

Det Sgt Napier said: "He stopped and turned and said 'Get back, I've got a gun,' and tapped his pocket. He then ran off but there was no sighting of a gun."

Just 40 minutes later at 6.30pm the man struck again at News Plus on East Street.

He threatened the husband and wife team behind the counter with a carving knife but they hit the panic alarm and he again made off empty-handed.

Det Sgt Napier said: "These are brave people. But it is not something we would recommend someone to do, to tackle an armed robber, because you don't know what is going to happen."

In the first attack the robber is described as a black man, 6ft 0ins tall. In the second he is described as about 5ft 11ins, of medium build, aged 25-30, with short Afro hair.

In both robberies a dark saloon car was seen, possibly a Renault Clio or a Toyota.

Anyone with any information is asked to contact police on 01206 762212 or Crimestoppers in confidence on 0800 555111.

ke victim Carl Holmes clearly enjoyed the spectacle – despite the rain. [8604-8]

Carl suffered a massive stroke while weight ['s home.
family was warned he would not probably not

· paralysed and needing a ventilator and 24 ught back, slowly regaining his sight, ability to speech.
red for at Beckingham Court rehabilitation unit

ned launched the Computer for Carl Appeal to nce achieved computer to improve his quality

ever-popular cyclamen is not a very reliable repeat performer and like the poinsettia will be coming to the end of its run.
Again water should be withheld with the plant stood in a shady corner outside until August when an attempt to rekindle life should be made. Weekly feeds and a lighter position with a move indoors by mid-September may prove fruitful. Some you win, some you may lose.
Azaleas are probably the best bet, given their particular requirements of occasional overhead misting, an assurance that they do not get dry and the occasional feed. Outdoors from the end of May until mid-September with the pot sunk up to its rim is a fairly reliable path to success.
Once indoors full light and a

compost is used.
Spathyllium floribundum, the Peace Lily, has become an increasingly familiar subject of late, doubtless due to its almost continuous show of flower with the absolute minimum of the customary slight troubles.
Division of these now may well be the answer to those too leafy for their containers.
The foliage begonias begin to stir at this time producing fresh new foliage giving the opportunity to remove the old and in some cases part into several new plants.
Fuchsias, pelargoniums and geraniums are usually better if all the old compost is removed and the roots trimmed back before giving a smaller pot to become re-established and a later move into the original one.

JOBS FOR THE WEEKEND

SNIP off hydrangea heads cutting down to the first pair of leaves.
Old overgrown plants may have some of their spent growths cut back to ground level.

THE main sowings of summer vegetables should now be put in hand.
Marrows, cucumbers and melon seed sown now and stood in a warm propagator or windowsill should yield plants of sufficient size for planting in cold frame or outdoors by the first week in June, the earliest safe time for planting

DIVIDE overgrown clumps of agapanthus. Often the use of a knife will be more helpful than the traditional two fork method.

ONKEY BUSINESS – ert Mead and Tania Cocksedge get a little help rom Sharon Asplin. [8603-31a]

MY NOW!

get gardening WITH JIM PEARCE

POT CARE – the Christmas poinsettia and a host of other pot plants are now looking for a little care and attention.

It's time to give those pot plants a treat

SHAKE off those winter blues from the houseplants and give a new impetus of life to old friends.
The Christmas poinsettia, cyclamen, azalea and perhaps a late flowering orchid along with a host of others are now looking for a refit.
By this time the poinsettia has lost much of its lustre, though some try to keep the pot boiling it is a plant that benefits from a complete rest and should have a total period of drying out.
Where the idea is to get a repeat performance after a rest until early July, the plant may be watered when new growth will follow almost overnight. Prune back hard to a newly-emerging shoot.
Keep in a full light position under glass feeding weekly with a tomato

continuance of misting should be the form. If the plant looks a little overbalanced for the size of the pot shift to a slightly larger size when first moving outside.
Use only the purpose-made ericaceous compost.
Orchids, particularly the cymbidiums, have gained in popularity of recent years. Their great asset is the longevity of their flowers. Where a plant is about to buckle or break the pot due to its very size, repotting may be considered and now would be the ideal time.
That said they should always be left until that stage has been reached, they like it that way.
From late May until August they may be stood outdoors in a lightly shaded spot and given an occasional feed of Maxicrop sprayed over the foliage. When re-potting ensure that only orchid

182

COMPUTER FOR CARL APPEAL

Generous readers offer cash and help

County Standard staff are rising to Army challenge

HAVE you ever wanted to get your own back on the staff at the Essex County Standard?

Well, now's your chance.

In a bid to raise money for our Computer for Carl Appeal we have taken on the challenge laid down by the Army – to complete their gruelling assault course.

And we are asking you, our readers, to sponsor us.

So, if you have fumed at some of the stories or pictures we've published in the past, your time for revenge has come.

For we will be forced to try to scale a 15ft high wall, swing across monkey bars, leap across ditches of water – without getting wet – crawl through pipes and keep our heads as we walk the plank and rope bridge, high above the spectators.

An elite team – sort of – from the County Standard aims to compete the course on Friday April 28.

Anyone who would like to sponsor us please complete the form below.

For ease of administration we would ask you to send in the money with the form and, of course, we promise to refund it if we fail.

Please make any cheques payable to Computer for Carl Appeal and send them to Computer for Carl Appeal, Essex County Standard, Oriel House, 43-44 North Hill, Colchester, Essex, CO1 1TZ.

GIVE THEM ENOUGH ROPE – County Standard staff have a sneak preview of the Army assault course which they intend to complete to raise money for the computer for Carl Appeal. Pictured are sub-editor John Renton and reporter Sharon Asplin giving acting editor Neal Harrington a push.
Picture
STEVE BRADING

HOW YOU CAN HELP

YOU can also send a donation or arrange a fund raising event on Carl's behalf. Contact reporter Sharon Asplin on 01206 508277 or send a donation to:
Computer for Carl Appeal, Essex County Standard, Oriel House, 43 North Hill, Colchester, CO1 1TZ, or take it to Barclays Bank, High Street, Colchester, and ask for the Computer for Carl Appeal, sort number 20-22-69, account number 00230332.
Cheques should be made payable to Computer for Carl Appeal.

ESSEX COUNTY STANDARD STAFF'S ARMY CHALLENGE SPONSORSHIP FORM

ESSEX COUNTY STANDARD

Name ....

....

....

Full address ....

Amount per obstacle _____ (15 in total)

Total amount donated £_____

Businessman donates £450 software package to appeal

Words: SHARON ASPLIN
Pictures: STEVE BRADING

THE Computer for Carl Appeal has received another welcome boost this week.

A second businessman from West Bergholt visited our offices this week to drop off £459-worth of software equipment for Colchester stroke victim Carl Holmes.

The man, who wanted to remain anonymous, has donated the Dragon Naturally Speaking Professional software needed to make the computer voice-activated.

This particular system has been recommended by medical experts as the best to help Carl.

The businessman said: "I wish him luck with it – I cannot imagine the trauma that he has gone through.

"We all think of stroke victims as being pensioners and it is unusual to read about it happening to a 26-year-old.

"But I totally admire his resilience and your appeal."

Our appeal's grand total now stands at £2,417.23, not counting the value of the equipment which has already been donated.

Three years ago Carl suffered a massive stroke while weight training at his cousin's home.

It left him so ill his family was warned he would not probably not survive.

But, although now paralysed and needing a ventilator and 24-hour care, Carl has fought back, slowly regaining his sight, ability to eat and drink and his speech.

He is now being cared for at Beckingham Court rehabilitation unit in Tolleshunt Major.

The County Standard launched the Computer for Carl Appeal to provide him with a voice-activated computer to improve his quality of life.

TAILOR MADE CONSERVATORIES

A AND K

Come and Visit our Showroom at:

A & K House, Main Road, Alresford, Colchester, Essex

WITH THE ADDED STRENGTH OF... TRICEPT

TEL: 01206 823903

£10,000 environment boost

MORE than £10,000 is being handed over to fund environmental projects at schools, councils and other groups across the county.

The money, which will be used to improve the quality of life and environment, has come from Essex County Council's Agenda 21 Millennium Fund.

More than 20 groups have been awarded grants ranging from £150 to £1,000.

Included are plans to create ponds, wildlife areas, woods, hedgerows and nature trails.

Those receiving money include Heathlands Primary School, in West Bergholt, BTCV Tiptree Group, in Tiptree, Kelvedon St Mary's School, Peters C of E Primary School in Coggeshall and Mistley Norman Primary School.

Co-o
real

by SHARON ASPLIN

A COLCHESTER store
ity has brought a bea
to the face of Colche
victim Carl Holmes.

After reading of Carl's
County Standard, the Co
East Essex Co-operati
decided to give him a tel
video recorder.

Co-op staff were anxious t
some entertainment now h
into Beckingham Court
unit in Tolleshunt Major.

Lorraine Collins, the society
tions officer, handed over t
Philips model to Carl on Mond

PLEASED

She said: "The Society is pl
towards improving Carl's qual

"He was so delighted to wa
Fools and Horses videos an
we've been able to make a diff

Carl was overjoyed with the
larly now he can catch up v
David Jason on screen.

The Essex County Standar

ON YOUR MARKS
– the County Standard
team from the top:
John Renton, Robert
Mead, Staff Glover,
Tania Cocksedge and
Sharon Asplin. (8603-8a)

QUICK MARCH – the team dash home after the obstacles. (8604-3)

YOU'RE IN THE AR

p's TV gift proves dividend for Carl

Readers' donations boost appeal for stroke victim, 26

generos-
ing smile
er stroke

light in the
hester and
e Society
vision and

at Carl had
has moved
habilitation

public rela-
e combined
y.

ased to help
ty of life.
ch his Only
d it's great
rence."
gift, particu-
th his hero

s Computer

for Carl Appeal stood at £2,367 late yesterday afternoon, thanks to our kind-hearted
readers' incredible generosity.

Cheques, large and small, have continued
to come to our office throughout the week.

This means we will soon be able to provide Carl with the voice-activated computer he needs. This will help him write a
book about his experiences, as well as provide entertainment and perhaps eventually
allow him to start up in business.

Three years ago Carl suffered a massive
stroke while weight training at his cousin's
home.

It left him so ill his family was warned he
would probably not survive.

But, although now paralysed and needing
a ventilator and 24-hour care, Carl has
fought back, slowly regaining his sight,
ability to eat and drink and his speech.

The County Standard launched the Computer for Carl Appeal to provide him with a
voice-activated computer to improve his
quality of life.

HOW YOU CAN HELP

TO send a donation or arrange
a fundraising event on Carl's
behalf, contact reporter Sharon
Asplin on 01205 508277 or send
a donation to:

Computer for Carl Appeal,
Essex County Standard, Oriel
House, 43 North Hill, Colchester, CO1 1TZ, or take it to Barclays Bank, High Street, Colchester, and ask for the
Computer for Carl Appeal, sort
number 20-2-69, account
number 00230322.

Cheques should be made payable to Computer for Carl
Appeal.

ALL SMILES – a delighted Carl
Holmes tries out his new
combined television and video
– a gift from the Colchester and
East Essex Co-operative
Society. He is pictured with
Lorraine Collins, the society's
public relations officer, who
handed it over on Monday.

Picture:
STEPHANIE MACKRILL
(7860-a)

County Standard staff rise to assault course challenge for Carl

IT rained.

The ground was soggy and the towering obstacles slippery.

And then it rained some more.

But our team from the Essex County Standard was undaunted and passed the challenge set down by the Army to tackle their assault course.

Five of us completed the challenge at the Colchester Garrison – reporters Sharon Asplin, Tania Cocksedge and Robert Mead, sub-editor John Renton and music writer Staff Glover – and lived to tell the tale.

And all proceeds from the event on Friday afternoon will go to our Computer for Carl Appeal, which is raising money to buy the Colchester stroke victim a voice-activated computer.

And not only did we help raise the cash, we also gave Carl himself an hour of side-splitting entertainment as he and staff from the Beckingham Court rehabilitation unit in Tolleshunt Major were on the sidelines cheering on our efforts to tackle the obstacles.

The obstacles included a 12-foot high wall, an elevated rope bridge and plank, water jumps and exhausting final sprint.

Three of the team even completed the course for a second time, helped by Army personnel, against the clock.

They finished in a respectable five minutes and 39 seconds – the record being just under three and a half minutes.

And our thanks go to Lieutenant Colonel (retired) Brian Davenport and Garrison Sergeant Major WO1 Tony Cartwright, who organised the assault course challenge.

Our team was helped on the day by 160 Army Youth Team, led by Colour-sergeant Pattison, who provided encouragement, safety tips, hot tea and a leg up in all the right places.

ALL SMILES – :

● THREE years training at his co... it left him so ill survive.

But, although hour care, Carl he eat and drink and He is now bein in Tolleshunt Ma

The County St provide him with of life.

OVER THE HURDLES – the team tackle the first obstacle.

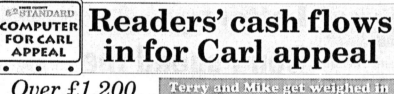

Readers' cash flows in for Carl appeal

Over £1,200 banked for stroke victim

GENEROUS readers have flocked to the aid of Colchester stroke victim Carl Holmes.

Within hours of the County Standard launching our Computer for Carl Appeal, the phones in our office were red-hot with promises of donations or inquiries about what could be done to help.

By yesterday a staggering £1,270 had been banked for 26-year-old Carl.

And one big-hearted reader has already come forward to drop off a printer for Carl.

The West Bergholt businessman, who did not wish to be named, was on the phone to us with his amazing offer just after 8am on Friday, the morning the appeal was officially launched.

And after we leapt at the chance to take the Hewlett Packard Deskjet 710C printer off his hands, he delivered it to our offices within the hour.

He said: "I had bought it for my

Other readers have already sent in £755 so far to our offices on North Hill, while by yesterday afternoon £515 more had been paid direct into the account at Barclays Bank.

This total includes one Colchester charity, which again did not want publicity, which donated £500 towards the target.

Its spokesman said: "Our charity are keen to help Carl improve his quality of life and will be delighted to give £500 towards the computer."

Carl finally arrived at Beckenham Court rehabilitation unit in Tolleshunt Major on Tuesday – the end of three months of complicated negotiations to have him cared for closer to home.

WARNED

Three years ago Carl suffered a massive stroke while weight training at his cousin's home.

It left him so ill his family was warned he would probably not survive.

But, although now paralysed and needing a ventilator and 24-

Terry and Mike get weighed in

IF you have blamed Colchester councillor Terry Sutton for the controversial changes in the High Street, well now's your chance to see him suffer!

For he has decided to reveal his most personal secrets to County Standard readers and embark on a sponsored slim for our Computer for Carl Appeal.

Mr Sutton, Colchester Council deputy leader and borough Liberal Democrat councillor for Berechurch, tipped the scales on Wednesday morning at 18 stone 12 pounds.

He aims to lose two stone in two months and has pledged the appeal £5 for every pound he sheds and £10 for every pound he misses his target weight by.

And he has signed up with Slimming World to help him trim down and resist the temptation of chocolate bars – his favourite snack.

BIKE

He said: "Hopefully through their careful attention I can realistically lose this weight and help Carl and myself at the same time.

"I am going to follow their diets and take up more exercise – the councillor responsible for transport policy will quite literally be getting on his bike!"

Joining him is the leaner Mike Chaplin, Essex County Newspapers sub-editor, who has less to lose – he wants to shave a stone off his 11-stone frame

on sale here

covered' it was not compatible, although it works with standard PCs.

"I was going to take it back or trade it in but I saw the paper's appeal and thought it would be good to give it to a good home.

"I have a son myself who is 24 and it will be great if something good can come out of this.

"It is brand new and has never even printed a page."

slowly regaining his sight, ability to eat and drink, speech and, above all, his sense of humour.

The County Standard launched the Computer for Carl Appeal to provide him with a voice-activated computer to improve his quality of life.

Carl said: "I just want to thank the County Standard and everything everyone is doing to help me. It is wonderful to know so many people care."

much more sensibly and cut out snacking before I go to bed as well as my alcohol intake.

"But I will be out on my bike three or four times a week, put more vigour into my badminton, and perhaps do a bit more walking."

He is collecting sponsorship from colleagues, family and friends and will also pledge £10 for every pound he does not lose from his target.

● Watch this space next month for a progress report.

SCALING NEW WEIGHTS – Colchester Council deputy leader Terry Sutton (right) and Essex County Newspapers sub-editor Mike Chaplin, watched by reporter Sharon Asplin, find out the dreaded truth as they prepare themselves for a sponsored slim for the Computer for Carl Appeal. *Picture: STEVE ARGENT (7972-1)*

HOW YOU CAN HELP

TO send a donation or arrange a fundraising event on Carl's behalf, contact reporter Sharon Asplin on 01206 508277 or send a donation to: Computer for Carl Appeal, Essex County Standard, Oriel House, 43 North Hill, Colchester, CO1 1TZ, or take it to Barclays Bank, High Street, Colchester, and ask for the Computer for Carl Appeal, sort number 20-22-69, account number 00230332.

Cheques should be made payable to Computer for Carl Appeal.

HELP GIVE CARL A VOICE

HOW WE HELPED

LEFT: – how we launched the appeal in last week's Essex County Standard.

Dancers – get in line for Carl!

DANCERS are being asked to get in line for Carl.

Kathy Kibble, who is a close family friend, is organising a line dance on Friday, May 5.

All proceeds will go to the Computer for Carl Appeal.

Mrs Kibble said: "Our families have always been very close and I thought this would be a great idea to raise

some money."

The event will be at the Queens Hall, Halstead, and generous caller Kym Barry from the Halstead Grapeviners is giving her services free of charge.

Tickets are £5 each. For details and to book call Mrs Kibble on 01787 475621 or Kym Barry on 01787 476508.

ENTERTAINER Bill Carter has offered his services to the Computer for Carl Appeal. One-man band Bill from Brightlingsea says he will provide 50s and 60s music, free of charge, to anyone wishing to organise a fundraising event for Carl. Call him on 01206 307004.

Words: SHARON ASPLIN   Picture: STEVE ARGENT

agic stroke victim Carl Holmes, 26, is moving closer

So happy to

BEFORE his accident Carl Holmes had always lived in Colchester, attending the Hazlemere infants and junior schools and then Sir Charles Lucas in Greenstead.

He was a quiet boy at school. When he grew up he became interested in horse racing and snooker. He never smoked and was teetotal.

Weight training was a fairly recent hobby and his family admit he went at it "a bit like a bull in a china shop".

But although this may have accelerated his accident, medical experts have said it was not the cause, which was a genetic weakness in the brain.

FOR Carl Holmes' mother Doreen Buxton the past three years have been hell.

But he would never have guessed it because every time she made the long journey to visit him in Stoke Mandeville Hospital she was always determined to greet him with a joke and a smile.

"It's been terrible," she admits. "What was really destroying was in the beginning when they said he would not survive it.

"For the first few months we just kept wondering what we were going to see.

"At times the hospital would ring up and say he was unconscious and we would have to travel all that way, worrying about what would happen when we arrived."

Doreen, 48, said it was made particularly harrowing as she and the family tried to put on a brave front for Carl.

"I go in there telling him jokes to keep him laughing and I'm sure people think we're a bit strange. But I could never go in there and shed tears because that would make it ten times worse for him.

"We've got to accept the injury he has got and that there is no cure – I was very upset the other week when he rang to tell me that he had thought when he left the hospital he would be walking and would be better.

"He said 'but I'm not, am I?'"

But there have been positive milestones. Doreen remembers fondly how three months after the accident he learned to eat again, choosing to tuck into a chicken nugget from the hospital canteen.

Three months after that he learned to cough again and last autumn his vision

CARING STAR – Top actor David Ja: has followed Carl's progress.

returned in one eye.

"There are slight improvements all time – all these are all things we take granted but for Carl they are j miraculous."

Stepfather Martin, 46, a school careta in Great Baddow, adds: "People who see C now think this is how he was after the str but he has come on a long way since then.

"It took us almost two years to accept way he is, to accept the fact he will not getting up again."

ESSEX COUNTY STANDARD
COMPUTER FOR CARL APPEAL

Help us to give Carl a voice in the world

will receive all the medical care he needs at Becking-Court.

what his family want to ensure is that he can have of the extras to improve his quality of life.

I a voice-activated computer is what the experts amend.

Carl does not have the use of his hands this will e him to complete his dream – to write a book to his experiences with others.

n Doreen said: "It took a long time for him to learn to gain and we did not really know if he ever actually I. When he first managed it, it was like a scream.

just wants to put his feelings down on paper and tell e what he has been through."

et Ashton, Essex Rivers Healthcare Trust head injury

Parents battle to bring son home

EXCLUSIVE: T

CON

FLASHBACKS – how the County Standard helped highlight Carl's plight. Left: Februar

County Standard campa

THE County Standard has been at the forefront of the fight to bring Carl home.

Back in March 1999 we ran an appeal for help to find him somewhere to live in the Colchester area, somewhere that could care for his needs but at the same time provide the right environment for him to be happy.

His family were distraught when it seemed the only suitable care for him would be somewhere in the south of

England, even further away from than Stoke Mandeville Hospital

But management at Beckingham rehabilitation unit in Tolleshunt came forward when they saw his ap the County Standard offering him a l

Even then it was not straightfo Complicated negotiations had to b ried out between the various authorities, the family and the ho ensure everything was suitable fo

188

be back!

IN THE PICTURE – the family of stroke victim Carl Holmes, Kelly 11, Lucy, 8, an· Doreen Buxton with grandmother Doreen Goodwin, look at a photograph of T' favourite David Jason who visited Carl in hospital.

ndard helps get tragic Carl back to Essex

ING HOME

l999. Above: August 13, 1999.

;ned for move

m   But the waiting paid off and his care will be paid for by North Essex Health rt   Authority.
or   Doreen cannot wait until Carl is safely in   in Tolleshunt Major. Instead of a long e.   drive away, he will be just 15 minutes d.   from her home.
ir-   She said: "I just want to thank the Essex th   County Standard for making this possible. to   They were the only ones at that time who   seemed to be listening."

Warm welcome awaits in Tolleshunt Major

STAFF at Carl's new home have already fallen in love with him.

Alison Rich, nurse manager of Beckingham Court rehabilitation unit in Tolleshunt Major, has already been to visit him four times in Stoke Mandeville and cannot wait until he arrives at the home on Tuesday.

She said: "We have already hit it off. But he's an easy guy to get along with – he's so easy going and has a great sense of humour."

It was Alison who saw the original story in the County Standard last March appealing for a home for Carl.

family, Beckingham Court and Essex Riv ers Healthcare Trust, which had pledged t pay for whatever care was appropriate.

A few structural changes have had to l carried out at the unit to enable a ceilin hoist to be fitted for Carl and the staff hav been given additional training to cope wit his needs.

And Alison admitted there had been quit a few last minute jobs to ensure everythin was ready.

"There have been calls about equipmen dealing with workmen," she said. "We hav also painted his room because he didn want pink so it is now a nice light blue.

Tender love – and care

Building a loving relationship is difficult enough, but for disabled people in residential care and in the community, it can be even more challenging. Rod Hermeston reports

hen Carl Holmes fell for his care worker, he knew there might be problems with her employers.

He was thrilled when she told him she felt the same. But sure enough, his residential care providers frowned on the relationship.

The couple stuck to their guns. Diane, 34, said she would leave if they were not allowed to continue seeing each other.

Carl, 28, who needs 24 hour support and relies on a ventilator, now lives in a bungalow in Colchester provided by a different provider, the charity John Grooms.

They see each other regularly and if Diane stays over, she takes on caring responsibilities for Carl.

"We just clicked, really. It is very good," he says.

Carl has his bungalow through the Treetops High Dependency Centre which also

Cheshire home in 1998.

Marion, 67, of Newcastle, has cerebral palsy. She claims relationships were not encouraged there and that staff would start laughing if she and the man in question started kissing.

"Things were just a bad when he moved into a bungalow. I was not allowed to stay beyond ten o'clock," she says.

She has since moved out and married another man, Paul.

The charity says that its staff are trained to support relationships and the sexual needs of its clients. It has 2,000 residential places and 12,000 clients in the community.

Fiona Stuart, director of services at Leonard Cheshire, says: "There are a significant number of service users living in our residential services that are having relationships with other service users, people in the community and with staff.

"We have examples of service

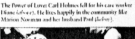

Picture: London Action on Disability.

She says: "There was no privacy. Staff were in and out of their rooms."

Concerns remain about the social care sector in general.

Anne MacEachen, a disability equality trainer, says staff in any care home can stop disabled people from having

The Power of Love: Carl Holmes fell for his care worker Diane (above r). He lives happily in the community like Marion Norman and her husband Paul (below).

provides residential care.

Sheila Flynn, centre nurse manager, says: "Our attitude is if somebody wants to conduct a relationship with a member of the opposite sex or the same sex, it is their own business."

But she concedes that John Grooms, too, does not encourage relationships between clients and members of staff.

Marion Norman had a relationship while in a Leonard

users visiting prostitutes. They have been given the support to do that." But staff cannot make the arrangements.

While she admits the charity has only 24 double rooms in residential settings, she says double beds have been put in other rooms.

Lack of double rooms was a problem identified by Angela Smith while researching experiences of disabled women living in care in 1997 for

relationships. "They can't sit them next to the person they want to talk to."

Only a few years ago, she says, she met a couple who were told they could not buy an engagement ring by staff.

Simon Parritt, director of the Association to Aid the Sexual and Personal Relationships of People with a Disability (SPOD) says: "Staff don't really know how to handle relationships in residential homes."

DN's telephone counsellor Lin Berwick comments:

"Many issues within a disabled person's life can prevent them from having a relationship, such as privacy, freedom of choice and pain. In a residential setting, carers can be over zealous with their need to control and protect. But life is about risk taking and making

choices, and learning from those choices, especially when they have been the wrong ones.

My role as a counsellor is to empower people with disabilities, but all too often I am dealing with the emotional consequences of disempowerment. One such example was a male in residential care who became very attached to his

female carer. The only time he had ever experienced intimacy and sexual arousal was while she washed and dressed him. They realised they were in love and so as not to compromise her position at work, she left the home. But his parents got involved, forbidding the relationship because they were worried about her motives he had received a large compensation settlement.

Another difficult issue is

pain. A woman with arthritis contacted me. She thought she was lesbian when she fell for her female carer. I felt the problem might have been that she was never allowed loving contact with anyone else. She didn't know if she was gay or if she simply needed to express loving feelings.

When a person experiences pain, as with severe arthritis, they often don't know what it is like to be cuddled or caressed

SPOD gets calls from staff worried about an inexperienced resident getting into a relationship or concerned about what will happen if relationships fail.

But it gets more calls from people in the community and their care staff asking, for

example, how much support they should give.

There is no doubt that there is a long way to go before disabled people living in care and many in the community can have the relationships that others take for granted.

because it is too painful.

Much of what I hear as a counsellor has to do with lack of knowledge and information in these areas. Why is it assumed that if you sit in a wheelchair, you are sexually dead from the neck down? When are we going to look at a person as a whole, beyond their disability, and try to help them reach their potential?"

If you would like to share your experience with Lin, see contact details on page 30.